DON WEEKES

THE GREAT
GRETZKY
TRIVIA BOOK

GREYSTONE BOOKS

Douglas & McIntyre Publishing Group

Vancouver/Toronto/New York

For Caroline, Kaitlyn and Alexandra—the greatest first line in my life

Text copyright © 1999 by Don Weekes

99 00 01 02 03 5 4 3 2 1

Greystone Books
A division of Douglas & McIntyre Ltd.
2323 Quebec Street, Suite 201
Vancouver, British Columbia
Canada V5T 4S7

Canadian Cataloguing in Publication Data
Weekes, Don
  The great Gretzky trivia book
  ISBN 1-55054-752-6
  1. Gretzky, Wayne, 1961– 2. National Hockey League—Miscellanea. I. Title.
GV848.5.G78W43 1999   796.962'64'092   C99-910719-4

Editing by Michael Carroll
Cover design by Peter Cocking
Typesetting by Brenda and Neil West, BN Typographics West
Cover photography by John Giamundo
Printed and bound in Canada by Transcontinental Printing
Printed on acid-free paper ∞

Every reasonable care has been taken to trace the ownership of copyrighted visual material. Information that will enable the publisher to rectify any reference or credit is welcome.

The publisher gratefully acknowledges the assistance of the Canada Council for the Arts and of the British Columbia Ministry of Tourism, Small Business and Culture. The publisher also acknowledges the financial support of the Government of Canada through the Book Publishing Industry Development Program for its publishing activities.

Canadä

Don Weekes is an award-winning television producer and writer with CFCF 12 in Montreal. This is his 14th hockey trivia quiz book.

CONTENTS

PREFACE

We've seen that little dance of Wayne Gretzky's a thousand times. After a goal, he celebrates by kicking his left foot high in the air and bringing his right arm down, as if he's pulling on a train whistle. We grew up watching that move game after game, but where did Gretzky get it from? The dance was borrowed from a player named Dave Pay, whom Gretzky's father coached in a Junior B league.

The Wayne Gretzky story is packed with such anecdotes. His rise from pipsqueak hockey player to sports legend in our time is classic. He didn't have a hard shot or skate very fast. And he was small by hockey standards. No, Gretzky's genius for goal scoring and play-making came from his on-ice vision and imagination. He could antic-ipate better than anyone, and his artful presence made everyone, both teammates and opponents, play better.

For us, the fans, if it wasn't his once-in-a-lifetime scoring feats that were astonishing, then it was those scoring credentials combined with his personality that made him so unique. As Gretzky often said, "No player is bigger than the game." Clearly, only No. 99 could say that and include everyone who has ever laced up skates and stickhandled a puck.

Gretzky had the kind of career no one thought was possible. He set standards—many of which will never be broken—in every scoring category. His moniker, the Great One, was earned not only by the number of records he smashed but by how they were smashed. Mau-rice Richard's 50-in-50 benchmark for snipers was demolished by Gretzky in 39 games. Phil Esposito's almost-unbelievable regular-season tally of 76 goals was topped by Gretzky with a heart-pounding 92-goal drive in 1981–82. Total points? No player in National Hockey League history had ever netted a 200-point season; Gretzky recorded a multitude of them. More remarkable, his career assists are greater than the combined career goals and assists of any other single player.

As great as Gretzky's achievements were, perhaps his most impor-tant contribution was his passion. He loved the game no less when he retired than when he first skated on his famous backyard rink in Brantford, Ontario, where he used to pay boyhood friends a nickel each to tend goal so he could take practice shots. In true Gretzky fashion, he always gave as much as he got from the game.

No one ever played hockey like No. 99. Welcome to *The Great Gretzky Trivia Book.*

DON WEEKES
JUNE 1999

Visit my Web site at: **www3.sympatico.ca/don.weekes/**

1

WAYNE'S WORLD

Wayne Gretzky wore a number of different skates during his career, Daoust, CCM and Nike among others. They were sharpened before every game (but not before practice). What kind of blade? "I've always used a Perfecta blade," reports No. 99. His laces? Always 90 inches for a better fit. In our opening chapter of general questions, we cover a wide range of Gretzky topics. Stay sharp, because anything is possible in Wayne's World.

(Answers are on page 6)

1.1   What was the No. 1 hockey rule Walter Gretzky taught his son, Wayne?
A. Practice, practice, practice
B. Go where the puck's going, not where it's been
C. Don't get bigheaded
D. When taking a pass, keep your head up

1.2   What role did little-known Sault Ste. Marie Greyhounds player Brian Gualazzi play in Wayne Gretzky's famous decision to wear No. 99 for the first time?
A. Gualazzi taped an extra nine on Gretzky's practice jersey
B. Gualazzi was already wearing the Greyhounds' No. 9 (Gretzky's favorite number)
C. Gualazzi threatened Gretzky if he asked for No. 9
D. Gualazzi was the first Greyhound to wear a number higher than 33

1.3   Against which NHL franchise did Wayne Gretzky score the most goals?
A. The Calgary Flames
B. The Carolina Hurricanes–Hartford Whalers
C. The Phoenix Coyotes–Winnipeg Jets
D. The Vancouver Canucks

1.4 How much did the World Hockey Association's Edmonton Oilers pay to acquire the rights to Wayne Gretzky in 1978?
A. Less than $1 million
B. $1 million
C. $2 million
D. $3 million

1.5 In what year did Wayne Gretzky score his 3,000th combined regular-season and playoff point?
A. 1995–96
B. 1996–97
C. 1997–98
D. 1998–99

1.6 What important hockey site is located at 42 Varadi Avenue?
A. The childhood home of Wayne Gretzky
B. The arena where Wayne Gretzky scored his first goal
C. Northlands Coliseum in Edmonton
D. The sports facility where Wayne Gretzky first met Gordie Howe

1.7 Which tough guy did the Edmonton Oilers first ice to police Wayne Gretzky's line?
A. Marty McSorley
B. Dave Semenko
C. Lee Fogolin
D. Kevin McClelland

1.8 Against which team did Wayne Gretzky score his famous 50th goal in 39 games in 1981–82?
A. The Montreal Canadiens
B. The Boston Bruins
C. The Vancouver Canucks
D. The Philadelphia Flyers

1.9 Which company did Wayne Gretzky and the great Russian goalie Vladislav Tretiak endorse together on television?
  A. Coca-Cola
  B. American Express
  C. Gillette
  D. Pro-Set Table-Top Hockey

1.10 When did Wayne Gretzky first start tucking part of his hockey sweater into his pants?
  A. In Brantford Atom League
  B. With the Toronto Young Nations in Junior B
  C. With the Sault Ste. Marie Greyhounds in Junior A
  D. In the WHA

1.11 Which kind of helmet did Wayne Gretzky wear?
  A. CCM
  B. Jofa
  C. Winn Well
  D. Cooper

1.12 Who was Wayne Gretzky's boyhood idol?
  A. Maurice Richard
  B. Gordie Howe
  C. Bobby Hull
  D. Bobby Orr

1.13 Where is Wayne Gretzky's office?
  A. In the goalie crease
  B. Behind the opponent's net
  C. In the slot in front of the opponent's net
  D. At center ice

1.14 Which four-letter word does Wayne Gretzky's Toronto restaurant have in its telephone number?
  A. S-T-A-R
  B. P-U-C-K
  C. G-O-A-L
  D. B-E-S-T

1.15 How many pages did the 1998–99 New York Rangers team guide devote to Wayne Gretzky?
A. Four pages
B. Six pages
C. Eight pages
D. 10 pages

1.16 What did Wayne Gretzky do to his hockey stick in preparation for the 1998 Olympics?
A. He used white tape instead of his usual black tape
B. He lengthened his stick's shaft
C. He had special markings inscribed on his stick
D. He used a slightly shorter blade to conform to Olympic regulations

1.17 What was the name of the team that Wayne Gretzky organized and toured with in Europe during the NHL labor dispute in 1994–95?
A. The Great Gretzkys
B. The Ninety-Nines
C. Wayne Gretzky's 99 All-Stars
D. Wayne's Excellent Euro Adventure

1.18 How much did Wayne Gretzky pay for the 1910 Honus Wagner baseball trading card?
A. $151,000 U.S.
B. $251,000 U.S.
C. $351,000 U.S.
D. $451,000 U.S.

1.19 Which sweater number was Wayne Gretzky wearing when he scored his very first goal playing organized hockey at age six?
A. No. 9
B. No. 11
C. No. 16
D. No. 22

1.20 Besides No. 99, what was the only other jersey number worn by Wayne Gretzky in his professional career?
A. No. 9
B. No. 10
C. No. 20
D. No. 79

1.21 How much money did Wayne Gretzky receive in the 1996 lawsuit against the NHL for misappropriation of pension money?
A. $6.91
B. $69.17
C. $691.70
D. $6,917

1.22 On average, how much did attendance jump at the Great Western Forum in Los Angeles when Wayne Gretzky was traded to the Kings?
A. 2,000 fans
B. 3,000 fans
C. 4,000 fans
D. More than 5,000 fans

1.23 How many times did Wayne Gretzky and Gordie Howe play together on the same team?
A. Three times
B. Seven times
C. 11 times
D. It never happened

1.24 According to Wayne Gretzky, what percentage of his assists came from his setting up behind the net?
A. 20 per cent
B. 40 per cent
C. 60 per cent
D. 80 per cent

1.25 Considering Wayne Gretzky began his NHL career in 1979–80, in which season did he record his 5,000th career shot on goal?
A. 1992–93
B. 1994–95
C. 1996–97
D. 1998–99

1.26 What is Walter Gretzky's nickname for his son, Wayne?
A. Wayner
B. Wiener
C. Wayne-o
D. Gretz

WAYNE'S WORLD
Answers

1.1 **B. Go where the puck's going, not where it's been**
Wayne Gretzky's first and most important coach was his dad. The elder Gretzky taught his son about practicing, avoiding overconfidence and keeping his head up, but his No. 1 rule was: Know where the play is heading and be there. A little something called anticipation.

1.2 **B. Gualazzi was already wearing the Greyhounds' No. 9 (Gretzky's favorite number)**
As a kid, Wayne Gretzky's favorite jersey number, No. 9, was usually taken by an older player. When he joined the Sault Ste. Marie Greyhounds, the famous digit was worn by Brian Gualazzi. "No one ever asked me to give [No. 9] up," Gualazzi said, as quoted in *The Hockey News*. "Not that I would have. It was no issue. I was a veteran and Wayne was a rookie." So Gretzky donned No. 14 in training camp and No. 19 to start the 1977–78 regular season. It didn't work out, though. "I tried 14 and 19 at first, but the ones didn't feel quite right on my back," said Gretzky. Then Greyhounds coach Muzz MacPherson and

general manager Angelo Bumbacco suggested he wear two nines (No. 99), an idea borrowed from the New York Rangers' Phil Esposito, who was using double sevens (No. 77). As Gretzky recalled, "At first I said, 'No, that's too hotdoggish.' But they convinced me to wear it." On his first night, No. 99 scored two goals. It was a lock. Gretzky played one season with Gualazzi on the Greyhounds before moving on to the WHA in 1978–79. Gualazzi never played in the NHL, but he will forever be the No. 9 who unintentionally gave hockey its greatest jersey number, 99. Today Gualazzi is an assistant Crown attorney in Sault Ste. Marie.

1.3   C. The Phoenix Coyotes–Winnipeg Jets

During his 20-year NHL career, Wayne Gretzky scored at least one goal against all 27 teams he played against, but his easiest target was Edmonton's divisional rival, Phoenix-Winnipeg. The Coyotes-Jets gave up 79 goals, Gretzky's highest goal count against any NHL franchise. No. 99 recorded one four-goal game, three three-goal games, 16 two-goal games, and 34 single-goal matches against the club.

1.4   A. Less than $1 million

In 1978, after just eight games and six points with the Indianapolis Racers, 17-year-old rookie Wayne Gretzky (as well as Peter Driscoll and Eddie Mio) was sold for $850,000 by the team's owner, Nelson Skalbania, to Peter Pocklington of the WHA Edmonton Oilers. Skalbania had originally signed Gretzky to a personal-services contract ($825,000 for four years), but after losing $40,000 per game in Indianapolis, he severed his ties with Gretzky. Obviously that was a big mistake. Skalbania had a handshake deal with the Winnipeg Jets, but owner Michael Gobuty unwisely listened to his scouts, who said the Kid was too small and wasn't worth the money. Another big mistake. Shortly after, Gretzky inked a new contract with Pocklington at center ice before an Edmonton crowd at Northlands Coliseum. The contract expiry date was 1999, the year Gretzky eventually retired. "I remember when he got off that little jet I sent to get him," Pocklington recalled. "Here's this skinny little kid with peach fuzz. I thought, 'My God, I paid $850,000 for that.' Just kidding."

1.5 B. 1996–97

Wayne Gretzky snared his milestone 3,000th point on a Luc Robitaille goal in a 6–2 New York Rangers win against Montreal's Jocelyn Thibault on December 1, 1996. It was Gretzky's 1,473rd game, counting both regular-season and playoff contests. "I didn't even know it," Gretzky said. "Honest, I just saw it on TV."

Breakdown of Wayne Gretzky's 3,000th NHL Point							
Games		Goals		Assists		Total Points	
RS	PS	RS	PS	RS	PS	RS	PS
1,280	193	846	112	1,792	250	2,638	362
Totals	1,473		958		2,042		3,000

RS/Regular season, PS/Postseason

1.6 A. The childhood home of Wayne Gretzky

The house at 42 Varadi Avenue in Brantford, Ontario, earned a place in hockey lore because of the rink that Walter Gretzky installed in his backyard. It was where No. 99 learned to skate. The neighborhood kids used to call it Wally Coliseum.

1.7 B. Dave Semenko

Because of the way Wayne Gretzky saw the ice and the play developing, he was always hard to hit. But a few checks connected, particularly in the 1981 playoffs. The New York Islanders' Dave Langevin and Bryan Trottier slowed him down, so much so that he wasn't the same speedy player in the later games of the series. Enter linemate Dave Semenko. He proved to be just the policeman the Oilers sought to protect their greatest asset. The matchup not only benefited Gretzky but also Semenko, who said of his newfound scoring touch: "Pretty easy when 99 shoots it off your stick." But Gretzky, all 170 pounds, also fought back in a different way. "If a guy ran him, Wayne would embarrass that guy," said former Oiler Lee Fogolin, as quoted in *Sports Illustrated*. "He'd score six or seven points on him. I saw him do it night after night."

1.8 D. The Philadelphia Flyers
No player in NHL history had scored 50 goals in fewer than 50 games before Wayne Gretzky did in 1981–82. Maurice Richard and Mike Bossy had 50-in-50 marks in their respective eras, but it was Gretzky who finally broke through with a five-goal spree on December 30, 1981, against the Flyers' Pete Peeters. Gretzky's fifth goal, his 50th of the season, was an empty netter, but Peeters still revels in his role, despite the circumstances. "Wayne got what, five that night?" Peeters said, as quoted in *Sports Illustrated*. "Believe me, it could have been nine or 10. I have vivid memories of coming out, challenging him, stopping him. And he hit at least three pipes. I can still hear them ringing."

1.9 C. Gillette
Even without his skates, Wayne Gretzky has scored some major accomplishments, particularly as a spokesperson in the big-league world of   advertising. Over the years, he has done endorsements for McDonald's, Hudson's Bay, Campbell Soup, Zurich Financial and Coca-Cola. Perhaps one of his most memorable pitches was the Gretzky-Tretiak commercial for Gillette—the first North American TV ad to use a Soviet athlete. It featured a nose-to-nose matchup between two of hockey's greatest, playing ... tabletop hockey.

1.10 A. In Brantford Atom League
Ever since he began playing organized hockey, Wayne Gretzky tucked in his sweater. When No. 99 was a small fry at age six on a team of 10-year-olds, his big sweater kept catching the butt end of his stick. Walter Gretzky tried the simplest solution. "My dad did it so [the sweater] wouldn't look so big on me," said Gretzky. Later, in the NHL, he used Velcro to make sure his sweater tuck stayed put. "I always cut off the fight strap—even for the All-Star Game," he admitted.

1.11 B. Jofa
No NHLer was more photographed than Wayne Gretzky. On the ice, his Jofa 235 was as familiar to fans as his sweater tuck. The custom began in the WHA: "I wore a CCM helmet in Indianapolis.

A player in Edmonton told me to try [the Jofa] because it was so much lighter. I never wore anything else." At one point, in the early 1990s, the Great One found out that his trademark helmet was considered unsafe by the NHL. He fired back: "I've worn my helmet 17 years and now they're afraid I'm going to get hurt. It's a big issue to them, but I'm going to wear the helmet I always have. Let's see if they kick me off the ice."

1.12 B. Gordie Howe

Gordie Howe was the reason Wayne Gretzky originally wore No. 9, and when the famed digit wasn't available in the junior ranks, he switched to No. 99, a tribute to his boyhood hero and hockey's longtime greatest player. During the 1978–79 WHA All-Star Game, Howe and Gretzky, the oldest and youngest players on the ice, teamed up. Gretzky tucked in his jersey, as usual. From nowhere, a hand appeared and pulled the top back out. It was Gordie Howe. Before the game, Howe had somehow found a needle and thread, sewed up the sides of the jersey to make it fit properly, then handed it back to the rookie wonder. Gretzky never said a word about any of this. Who argues with a boyhood idol?

1.13 B. Behind the opponent's net

Wayne Gretzky's "office" on the ice was behind the net. The strategy started in Junior B hockey after Gretzky kept getting knocked over by big defensemen. At the suggestion of his coach, No. 99 began setting up behind the net, much as Bobby Clarke was doing with the Philadelphia Flyers. The net offered the smaller Gretzky not only protection but made defenders turn their backs to his teammates, causing breakdowns that led to Gretzky-assisted goals. Besides using the net to set up his slot man, Gretzky could deke out either way to make a pass or score on a wraparound.

1.14 B. P-U-C-K

The phone number for Wayne Gretzky's, No. 99's chow palace in downtown Toronto, is 979-PUCK. The address is 99 Blue Jays Way.

1.15 D. 10 pages

Every season NHL clubs publish team guides, complete with
regular-season and playoff records, franchise history and current-
player profiles. Each team member usually gets two pages devoted
to his career. In some cases, exceptions are made for players
such as Mark Messier, who receive four pages because of their
star power and contributions to hockey. Wayne Gretzky and
Mario Lemieux are on a higher level. In 1996–97, Lemieux's
retirement season, the Pittsburgh Penguins devoted eight pages
to the Magnificent One and his career. In the 1998–99 New
York Rangers guide, Gretzky was given a 10-page spread, high-
lighted by a year-by-year compendium of facts and statistics, as
well as a short biography, "The Legend of 99."

1.16 C. He had special markings inscribed on his stick

Wayne Gretzky took the Olympic symbol and created a new
design that incorporated his initials into the five rings. The art-
work was marked into the butt of his stick.

1.17 C. Wayne Gretzky's 99 All-Stars

While waiting for an end to 1994–95's NHL player lockout,
Gretzky organized Wayne Gretzky's 99 All-Stars, a team of all-
star friends that toured Europe for about a month. The flashy
red-and-white uniforms were covered with sponsorship logos
from Coca-Cola to L.A. Gear.

1.18 D. $451,000 U.S.

Originally bought for $451,000 in a partnership deal between former Los Angeles Kings owner Bruce McNall and Wayne Gretzky, the 1910 Honus Wagner baseball card is today owned 100 per cent by Gretzky, who bought McNall's half ownership of the card for $225,000 from bankruptcy trustees. Gretzky's Wagner card is considered to be the highest-graded card of the 40 Wagners in existence. The purchase price was the highest ever for a baseball card.

1.19 B. No. 11

Wayne Gretzky's first number in hockey wasn't No. 9 or No. 99. When he joined the minor-hockey program in Brantford as a six-year-old, his beloved No. 9 was taken (apparently by someone named Brian Queley), so he was handed No. 11. Spotting the older boys four years and quite a few pounds, he scored his one and only goal in his minor-hockey rookie year. According to Walter Gretzky, Wayne's dad, his famous son's first goal was scored at 18:51 of the first period. The number is notable, of course, because it was Gretzky's 1,851st point that moved him ahead of Gordie Howe as the NHL's all-time scoring leader.

1.20 C. No. 20

Wayne Gretzky wore only one other sweater number besides No. 99 during his entire pro career. It happened on November 3, 1978, in his first WHA game with the Edmonton Oilers. The Alberta team didn't have a jersey bearing his celebrated No. 99 ready, so Gretzky was handed No. 20. The number switch had little adverse effect: Gretzky scored his first Oilers goal in the club's 4–3 win over Winnipeg. In the next game, Gretzky donned his traditional double nines.

1.21 D. $6,917

In 1996 the Supreme Court of Canada ruled in favor of seven retired NHLers who filed a $40-million lawsuit against the league for lost pension money between 1947 and 1982. The lump-sum payments to 1,343 players was based on years of service, pension contributions and age. Gordie Howe received

$205,005, the most among all NHLers. Wayne Gretzky got $6,917 for his services prior to 1982.

1.22 D. More than 5,000 fans

Before Wayne Gretzky arrived in Los Angeles in 1988, the Kings averaged about 10,000 fans per game and were the NHL's worst-drawing team on the road. In Gretzky's seven full seasons in L.A., attendance rocketed to 15,700, or 98-per-cent capacity of the Forum, and L.A. became the No. 1 road attraction, playing to near-capacity every night. As a measure of the Great One's influence, his Kings were the only pro sports team in Southern California to sell out every home game in 1991–92.

1.23 A. Three times

Despite the 33-year age difference between Gordie Howe and Wayne Gretzky, their hockey careers did overlap for two seasons, providing opportunities for the pair to play opposite each other on numerous occasions, both in the WHA (1978–79) and the NHL (1979–80). Although they were never signed to the same franchise, they did play as teammates in the 1979 WHA All-Star series, a three-game round between the WHA's best and the Moscow Dynamo. Coach Jacques Demers centered Wayne between Gordie and his son, Mark, to produce the hottest line on the ice. The trio scored four goals to help sweep the series. On one play, Howe dug the puck out of the corner and slid a pass to Gretzky in the slot. It was as if the old man of 50 had been playing his entire career with the 17-year-old whiz kid. Gretzky and Howe also played in the NHL's 1980 All-Star contest. Howe and his Wales Conference teammates defeated the Campbell Conference and Gretzky, with a 6–3 score. Howe picked up an assist, while Gretzky went scoreless. It was Howe's 23rd and final All-Star appearance, and No. 99's first as an NHLer.

1.24 B. 40 per cent
Wayne Gretzky will probably be remembered first for his playmaking. When he was set up in his "office," someone usually scored a goal. "Forty per cent [of my assists] have come from behind the net," Gretzky once said. "The next biggest number would be hitting the late guy. Between those two plays, I'd say that probably accounts for three-quarters of my assists." Gretzky amassed 2,223 assists, including playoff helpers.

1.25 D. 1998–99
After being stuck at 4,999 career shots for three games in November 1998, Wayne Gretzky chalked up his 5,000th shot on November 27 against Pittsburgh's Tom Barrasso. He then scored goals in three straight games, including his 890th NHL career marker and his first against New York Islanders goalie Tommy Salo on December 2. (At the time, Salo was the only goalie with a minimum 10 appearances against Gretzky to blank No. 99). Gretzky fired a lifetime 5,089 shots in the NHL.

1.26 B. Wiener
Wayne Gretzky's dad tried a couple of nicknames on him before one stuck. Walter went from his son's given name to Wayner and finally to Wiener. The media christened him the Great One, but close friends simply call him Gretz.

GAME 1

CROSSWORD OF GREATNESS

(Solutions are on page 119)

Across

1, 3 and 7. The magazine that named Wayne Gretzky Man of the
   Year in 1981
9. Gretzky was never claimed in the 1979 Expansion ____
10. In 1983 Mattel introduced a Gretzky action ____
12. ____ Ross Trophy
13. Gretzky's longtime coach, John ____
15. Road ____
16. The ____ player in the world
19. Hometown of Gretzky's Ontario Hockey Association team, ____
   Ste. Marie
20. Gretzky friend and business partner, actor John ____
21. The Magnificent One
22. Gretzky's last team
25. The NHLer who injured Gretzky at the Canada Cup in 1991,
   ____ Suter
27. Gretzky's ____ to the Kings had Canada in an uproar
28. WHA ____ of the Year in 1978–79
30. Gretzky's OHA team name
31. Mrs. Gretzky
32. A seeing-eye ____
33. Gretzky played in 18 All-____ Games

Down

1. Players on the same side
2. In 1999 Gretzky came to the ____ of his career
3 and 14. Gretzky has four ____ ____ rings
4. Canadian province where Gretzky was born
5. Russian player who attended Gretzky's wedding, Vladislav ____
6 and 23. In Brantford Gretzky played for the ____ ____
7. Gretzky played 20 years in the ____

16

8. How writer Peter Gzowski characterized Gretzky's play: "like a ____"
11. Host of late-night show on which Gretzky appeared
17. Fame
18. Four-time winner of the Lady Byng ____
20. Gretzky on the cover of ____ *Aficionado*
24. Baseball team Gretzky played for in 1980, CKPC ____
25. Gretzky's idol, ____ Howe
26. ____ Glen Sather
27. Gretzky was still a ____ when he signed with Edmonton
29. Gretzky's NHL team before the New York Rangers

2

HISTORY IN THE MAKING

What is the only league-organized team for which Wayne Gretzky played but never scored a goal? In this chapter, we check out the scoring exploits of hockey's greatest marksman. Among No. 99's numerous team and league records, there are many personal firsts, including the only club he went goalless with in his career—the Peterborough Petes of the Ontario Hockey Association. On three occasions in 1976–77 (November 26, January 3 and March 3), he was called up from the Seneca Nationals Junior B team to join the Junior A Petes. Gretzky, a skinny 15-year-old center, registered three assists in three games, but no goals. He claims he never really had a good scoring opportunity. Another first. Check out these other Gretzky milestones that made scoring history.

(Answers are on page 24)

2.1 Against which team did Wayne Gretzky score his first professional goal?
  A. The Vancouver Canucks
  B. The Edmonton Oilers
  C. The Quebec Nordiques
  D. The Indianapolis Racers

2.2 What is the greatest number of goals scored by Wayne Gretzky in the first 50 games from the start of the season?
  A. 51 goals
  B. 56 goals
  C. 61 goals
  D. 66 goals

2.3 Against which NHL goalie did Wayne Gretzky score the most goals?
A. Hartford's Mike Liut
B. Vancouver's Kirk McLean
C. Minnesota's Don Beaupre
D. Vancouver's Richard Brodeur

2.4 When did Wayne Gretzky register his NHL-record 92-goal season?
A. 1981–82
B. 1982–83
C. 1983–84
D. 1984–85

2.5 In 1970–71, Phil Esposito fired an NHL high of 550 shots on net and scored a league-record 76 goals. How many shots did Wayne Gretzky need in 1981–82 to score 77 goals and break Espo's goal-scoring record?
A. 300 shots
B. 400 shots
C. 500 shots
D. 600 shots

2.6 How many shots on net did Wayne Gretzky take during his NHL-record 92-goal season in 1981–82?
A. 319 shots
B. 369 shots
C. 419 shots
D. 469 shots

2.7 How many of the top positions does Wayne Gretzky hold in the NHL record book for most assists in one season?
A. The top three positions
B. The top six positions
C. The top nine positions
D. The top 12 positions

2.8 How many points did Wayne Gretzky score during his 51-game point-scoring streak in 1983–84?
A. Less than 125 points
B. Between 125 and 150 points
C. Between 150 and 175 points
D. More than 175 points

2.9 What is the greatest number of games Wayne Gretzky has gone in his NHL career without scoring a goal?
A. 12 games
B. 15 games
C. 18 games
D. 21 games

2.10 In which league did Wayne Gretzky produce the greatest margin of points between himself and the next best player?
A. In minor hockey
B. In junior hockey
C. In the WHA
D. In the NHL

2.11 What was Wayne Gretzky's record in 18 regular-season games with the St. Louis Blues?
A. 5 goals + 6 assists = 11 points
B. 8 goals + 13 assists = 21 points
C. 11 goals + 20 assists = 31 points
D. 14 goals + 27 assists = 41 points

2.12 Wayne Gretzky scored so many assists each season that on a few occasions he could have won the NHL scoring race on assist totals alone. How many times did he accomplish this feat?
A. Never
B. Only once
C. Two times
D. Four times

2.13 Out of seven penalty shots awarded him, how many times did Wayne Gretzky score one-on-one in his career?
A. Only once
B. Three times
C. Five times
D. Seven times

2.14 What percentage of team goals did Wayne Gretzky score or assist on while playing with the Edmonton Oilers?
A. 38 per cent
B. 48 per cent
C. 58 per cent
D. 68 per cent

2.15 Considering that Wayne Gretzky began his NHL career in 1979–80, in what season did he score his 1,000th combined goal (regular season and playoff)?
A. 1995–96
B. 1996–97
C. 1997–98
D. 1998–99

2.16 How many NHL games did it take Wayne Gretzky to score 500 goals?
A. 525 games
B. 575 games
C. 625 games
D. 675 games

2.17 Wayne Gretzky topped the Edmonton Oilers in goal scoring six times in eight years. How often did he lead the Los Angeles Kings in goals during his seven seasons in Tinseltown?
A. Never
B. Once
C. Three times
D. Four times

2.18 How many goals did Wayne Gretzky score as an Edmonton Oiler and as a Los Angeles King to reach his record 802-goal mark?
A. 483 (Oilers) + 319 (Kings) = 802 goals
B. 503 (Oilers) + 299 (Kings) = 802 goals
C. 543 (Oilers) + 259 (Kings) = 802 goals
D. 583 (Oilers) + 219 (Kings) = 802 goals

2.19 If Gordie Howe was 40 years old when he scored his 700th career goal and Phil Esposito was 38, how old was Wayne Gretzky when he potted his 700th?
A. 36 years old
B. 34 years old
C. 32 years old
D. 30 years old

2.20 How many times did Wayne Gretzky break the 200-point plateau during his NHL career?
A. Once
B. Twice
C. Three times
D. Four times

2.21 What is the highest number of points Wayne Gretzky scored in one season, including the playoffs?
A. 225 points
B. 255 points
C. 285 points
D. 325 points

2.22 To reach his milestone 802-goal record, how many empty-net goals did Wayne Gretzky score?
A. 20 to 30 empty-net goals
B. 30 to 40 empty-net goals
C. 40 to 50 empty-net goals
D. More than 50 empty-net goals

2.23 What historic goal did Wayne Gretzky score on December 21, 1991?
   A. The goal that surpassed Maurice Richard's career total
   B. The goal that surpassed Bobby Hull's career total
   C. The goal that surpassed Phil Esposito's career total
   D. The goal that surpassed Marcel Dionne's career total

2.24 What is the record for most hat tricks (three-or-more-goal games) scored by one player in an NHL season?
   A. Six hat tricks
   B. 10 hat tricks
   C. 12 hat tricks
   D. 16 hat tricks

2.25 What was Wayne Gretzky's highest goals-per-game average in one season?
   A. 0.99 goals per game
   B. 1.18 goals per game
   C. 1.46 goals per game
   D. 2.20 goals per game

2.26 What is the greatest number of goals scored by Wayne Gretzky during a season, *including* the playoffs?
   A. 92 goals
   B. 96 goals
   C. 100 goals
   D. 104 goals

2.27 Which team was Wayne Gretzky playing for when he counted his 100th career playoff goal?
   A. The Edmonton Oilers
   B. The Los Angeles Kings
   C. The St. Louis Blues
   D. The New York Rangers

2.28 As of 1998–99, how many of Wayne Gretzky's 122 career playoff goals were game winners?
A. 6 of 122 goals
B. 12 of 122 goals
C. 18 of 122 goals
D. 24 of 122 goals

2.29 Upon his retirement in 1999, Wayne Gretzky had won more Art Ross Trophies than any other player. How many scoring crowns did Gretzky win?
A. Six scoring titles
B. Eight scoring titles
C. 10 scoring titles
D. 12 scoring titles

2.30 In what percentage of games did Wayne Gretzky score at least one point? (We're not looking for the points-per-game average.)
A. 62 per cent
B. 72 per cent
C. 82 per cent
D. 92 per cent

HISTORY IN THE MAKING
Answers

2.1 **B. The Edmonton Oilers**
Ironically the club that earned Wayne Gretzky his greatest fame, the Edmonton Oilers, is the same team he scored his first goal against. Before his NHL career began in 1979, Gretzky played the 1978–79 regular season split between the Indianapolis Racers (eight games) and the Edmonton Oilers (72 games) of the WHA. His first-ever professional goal came in his fourth pro start. It was anything but spectacular. Gretzky fanned on a weak backhand against Edmonton, the team he would later turn into an NHL dynasty. It happened on October 20, 1978, before 6,386 fans at Indianapolis's Market Place

Arena. Gretzky scored another goal in the 4–3 loss, which history recorded as his first multiple-goal game. Less than a year later, the Great One potted his first NHL goal against the Vancouver Canucks on October 14, 1979.

2.2 C. 61 goals

One of Wayne Gretzky's more obscure records is the league-high 61 goals he scored during Edmonton's first 50 games between October 8, 1981, and January 22, 1982. His awesome 1.22 goals-per-game average leveled off in the final 30 games of the 80-game schedule when he managed only a goal per game! As with many of his other records, Gretzky tied himself for first place in this category with another 61-goal tear in 1983–84.

Most Goals in 50 Games from Start of Season*			
Player	**Team**	**Duration**	**Goals**
Wayne Gretzky	Edm	10/07/81 to 1/22/82	61
Wayne Gretzky	Edm	10/05/83 to 1/25/84	61
Mario Lemieux	Pit	10/07/88 to 1/31/89	54
Wayne Gretzky	Edm	10/11/84 to 1/28/85	53
Brett Hull	St. L	10/04/90 to 1/26/91	52
Current to 1998–99			

2.3 D. Vancouver's Richard Brodeur

Wayne Gretzky scored on 155 NHL goalies in his career, most often against Richard Brodeur, who was victimized 29 times—more often than Mike Liut (25), Greg Millen (21), Don Beaupre (21) and Kirk McLean (21), the only goalies in the 20-goals-against range. Brodeur and Gretzky were so familiar with each other as Smythe Division neighbors that they maintained a certain rapport. "When I made a save against him, I'd say something like, 'Not this time!'" remembered Brodeur, as quoted in *Sports Illustrated*. "And he'd yell, 'I'll be back!'" Even in the WHA, Brodeur couldn't shake the Gretzky jinx. While tending goal for the WHA Quebec Nordiques, Brodeur gave up two more Gretzky goals (February 9 and March 7, 1979) in No. 99's first pro season, 1978–79.

2.4 A. 1981–82

Wayne Gretzky smashed a number of hockey's most important scoring records in 1981–82, the season, as Gretzky once said, "all heaven broke lose. Pucks started going into the net on their own. I'd tip 'em in, bounce 'em in, wobble 'em in, elbow 'em in, wish 'em in. No matter what I tried, they kept finding their way past goaltenders." In one four-game stretch, Gretzky scored 10 goals. He nailed the prestigious 50-goal mark in just 39 games, broke Phil Esposito's 76-goal record and became the first player to score 200 points in a season. Teamed with Finnish sniper Jari Kurri, Gretzky was the proverbial Energizer Bunny: he just kept going and going and going. His favorite victims were Los Angeles's Mario Lessard, whom he netted seven goals against, and Hartford's Greg Millen, Philadelphia's Pete Peeters and Calgary's Reggie Lemelin, all of whom he beat five times. No player in hockey has ever dominated a season the way Gretzky did in 1981–82.

2.5 A. 300 shots

Phil Esposito scored 76 goals on 550 shots in 1970–71. Wayne Gretzky broke Espo's 11-year-old record on his 300th shot, firing goal No. 77 of the season against Buffalo's Don Edwards on February 24, 1982.

2.6 B. 369 shots

To establish his NHL goal-scoring record of 92 goals in 1981–82, the Great One directed 369 shots on net in 80 games, an average of 4.6 shots per game or, incredibly, almost a goal on every fourth shot!

2.7 D. The top 12 positions

No record is more indicative of Wayne Gretzky's playmaking abilities than the number of assists he amassed in one season. Gretzky owns the first, second, third, fourth, fifth, sixth, seventh, eighth, 10th, 11th and 12th greatest assist seasons in league annals—each of 100 points or more, including his record 163 assists in 1985–86. Only Bobby Orr and Mario Lemieux have assisted on as many as 100 goals in one season.

2.8 **C. Between 150 and 175 points**
Wayne Gretzky had seven streaks of 20 or more consecutive games with at least one point during his career, but his best streak, an NHL record 51-game span, totaled an astonishing 61 goals and 92 assists for 153 points. It began on October 5, 1983, and continued uninterrupted for almost four months before Los Angeles Kings goalie Markus Mattsson finally shut down No. 99 on January 28, 1984.

2.9 **D. 21 games**
"The drought of '97," as it became known, turned into a goal-scoring dry spell without precedent in the 20-year history of hockey's greatest goal scorer. For 21 agonizing games (five games longer than his previous goalless streak) from December 30, 1996, to February 21, 1997, the Great One wasn't so great. Although he continued piling up assists to remain third in point totals, he experienced his worst goal slump. "As time goes by, it wears on you," he said. "You want to contribute more offensively." Tighter checking and Wayne's sore back were contributing factors. Gretzky's own theory? "At the beginning of the year, I concentrated on going to the net, and if it opens up, making the play," he explained. "Right now I'm trying to make the play and then go to the net." The drought ended on a 50-foot shot at 17:54 of the second period in a 7–2 New York Rangers loss against Hartford. It was Gretzky's 17th of 1996–97, his 854th NHL career goal and the 900th goal of his professional career.

2.10 **A. In minor hockey**
As a nine-year-old in 1970–71 with the Brantford Nadrofsky Steelers of the Ontario Minor Hockey Association, Wayne Gretzky scored 196 goals and 120 assists in 76 games. "He'll never do that again," people said. They were right. The next season the wonderboy racked up an astounding 378 goals and 139 assists for 517 points in 69 games. That season Gretzky won the novice-league scoring race by 238 goals.

2.11 B. 8 goals + 13 assists = 21 points
In 18 games for the St. Louis Blues, Wayne Gretzky scored 21 points. St. Louis acquired No. 99 from Los Angeles on February 27, 1996, for centers Patrice Tardif and Roman Vopat, left winger Craig Johnson and two draft picks (Peter Hogan in 1996 and Matt Zultek in 1997).

2.12 D. Four times
Wayne Gretzky led (or shared) the NHL in assists 16 times (13 consecutively). On four occasions, his assist numbers were so phenomenal that he tied or outscored his nearest rival's *point* totals and won the league scoring crown on assists alone. In two of those seasons, Gretzky's rival was his own linemate, Jari Kurri —a testament to the league-wide dominance of the Gretzky-Kurri line in Edmonton. Furthermore, in three of those years, No. 99 also led the league in goals.

Wayne Gretzky's Most Dominant Seasons				
Year	**Player**	**Goals**	**Assists**	**Totals**
1982–83	Wayne Gretzky	71	125	196
	Peter Stastny	47	77	124
1984–85	Wayne Gretzky	73	135	208
	Jari Kurri	71	64	135
1985–86	Wayne Gretzky	52	163	215
	Mario Lemieux	48	93	141
1986–87	Wayne Gretzky	62	121	183
	Jari Kurri	54	54	108

2.13 C. Five times
While the NHL penalty-shot success rate favors the goalie in 60 per cent of the shots, Wayne Gretzky reversed that trend. In seven attempts, the Great One scored five times, only twice being stopped by Washington's Pat Riggin on November 24, 1982, and Toronto's Peter Ing on January 5, 1991. Gretzky's success rate *mano a mano* is better than 71 per cent.

2.14 B. 48 per cent

In nine Edmonton Oilers seasons, Wayne Gretzky scored or assisted on a staggering 48 per cent of the team's 3,487 goals. The Great One scored 1,669 career points with Edmonton. His best percentage season was 1984–85 when he finished with 208 points to help the Oilers amass 401 team goals, a mind-numbing 52-per-cent share.

2.15 C. 1997–98

Combining goal totals from the regular season and the postseason, Wayne Gretzky lit his 1,000th red light on March 7, 1998, in a 6–3 loss to the New Jersey Devils. It was his 1,606th NHL match.

2.16 B. 575 games

As he did with many of his milestone goals, Wayne Gretzky scored his 500th quicker than anyone else in NHL history. No. 500 came against Vancouver on November 22, 1986, Gretzky's 575th game—a goals-per-game average of .869!

The NHL's Fastest 500-Goal Scorers*

Players	Date	Game No.	Goalie
Wayne Gretzky	Nov. 22, 1986	575	Empty net
Mario Lemieux	Oct. 26, 1995	605	Tommy Soderstrom
Mike Bossy	Jan. 2, 1986	647	Empty net
Brett Hull	Dec. 22, 1996	693	Stephane Fiset
Phil Esposito	Dec. 22, 1974	803	Jim Rutherford

* Current to 1998–99

2.17 A. Never

Although Wayne Gretzky enjoyed several productive seasons in Los Angeles, his goal production declined when he joined the Kings in 1988. Bernie Nicholls led the Kings in goals in Gretzky's first year in L.A. Luc Robitaille was top dog for the next five years, and Rick Tocchet was the leading sniper in the lockout-shortened 1994–95 season.

2.18 D. 583 (Oilers) + 219 (Kings) = 802 goals

Wayne Gretzky scored 583 goals—or 72.7 per cent of his 802 mark—with the Edmonton Oilers before his move to Los Angeles, where he netted another 219 goals (27.3 per cent). Between October 14, 1979, and March 23, 1994, No. 99 scored four five-goal games, nine four-goal games, 36 three-goal games, 141 two-goal games and 356 one-goal games.

2.19 D. 30 years old

As of 1999, only five NHLers had achieved 700-goal careers. Naturally Wayne Gretzky was the youngest to score goal No. 700 among the all-star group. The Great One was just 30 years old and in his 12th season.

The NHL's 700-Goal Club*				
Player	Team	Year	Season No.	Age
Gordie Howe	Detroit	1968–69	23rd	40
Phil Esposito	NYR	1979–80	17th	38
Marcel Dionne	LA	1987–88	17th	36
Wayne Gretzky	LA	1990–91	12th	30
Mike Gartner	Phoenix	1997–98	19th	38
Current to 1998–99				

2.20 D. Four times

Wayne Gretzky is the only NHLer to score 200 or more points in a season. Amazingly he did it four times in five years with Edmonton. In the fifth season, 1982–83, he "stumbled" and recorded 196 points. The Great One scored 212 points in 1981–82; 205 points in 1983–84; 208 in 1984–85; and in his best season, 1985–86, 215 points, to establish an NHL record. In those five years, Gretzky scored 1,036 points.

2.21 B. 255 points

In 1984–85, Wayne Gretzky totaled 208 points in 80 regular-season games, adding 47 points in 18 playoff games. This will probably be one of No. 99's most difficult records to break.

2.22 C. 40 to 50 empty-net goals
On his way to passing Gordie Howe's all-time record of 801 goals, Wayne Gretzky potted 46 empty-net goals. Among his most famous empty-netters are his career 100th, his 50th in 39 games and his 500th career goal.

2.23 D. The goal that surpassed Marcel Dionne's career total
As the NHL's all-time leader in goals, assist and points, Wayne Gretzky surpassed all of the game's greatest scorers. On December 21, 1991, he notched his 732nd goal to pass Dionne, the last sniper in his path before his assault on Gordie Howe's 801-goal record.

Wayne Gretzky's Milestone Goals

Career Goal No.	Date	Achievement
1	10/14/79	First NHL goal
50	04/02/80	First of eight straight 50-goal years
156	12/30/81	50 goals in 39 games
183	02/24/82	Scored 77th goal to break Phil Esposito's single-season record
198	03/26/82	Scored 92nd goal to set highest single-season total
325	01/18/24	Passed Nels Stewart's career-goal total
500	11/22/86	Passed Mike Bossy's record for fastest 500 goals
545	10/14/87	Passed Maurice Richard's career-goal total
611	12/23/88	Passed Bobby Hull's career-goal total
641	10/15/89	Set all-time points total: 1,851
718	03/28/91	Passed Phil Esposito's career-goal total
732	12/21/91	Passed Marcel Dionne's career-goal total
802	03/23/94	Passed Gordie Howe's career-goal total
894	03/29/99	Last NHL goal

2.24 B. 10 hat tricks

Among his scoring records, Wayne Gretzky holds the mark for the most three-or-more-goal games in one season. In 1981–82, he notched a record 10 hat tricks for Edmonton with six three-goal games, three four-goal games and one five-goal game. Mario Lemieux and Mike Bossy came close during their stellar careers. The pair tied for second spot with nine three-or-more-goal games in a season, but neither topped Gretzky, who amazingly pulled off another 10-hat-trick season two years later in 1983–84. Those two seasons, 1981–82 and 1983–84, were Gretzky's highest goal-scoring years (92 and 87 goals).

2.25 B. 1.18 goals per game

Not since the NHL's first season (1917–18) has anyone come close to Joe Malone's incredible average of 2.20 goals per game on 44 goals in 20 games. Although it's impossible to compare the two eras of hockey, the best mark among today's players is Wayne Gretzky's 1.18 average from 87 goals in 74 games in 1983–84.

The NHL's Modern-Day Goals-Per-Game Leaders*					
Player	Team	Season	Games	Goals	Average
Wayne Gretzky	Edm	1983–84	74	87	1.18
Wayne Gretzky	Edm	1981–82	80	92	1.15
Mario Lemieux	Pit	1992–93	60	69	1.15
Mario Lemieux	Pit	1988–89	76	85	1.12
Brett Hull	St. L	1990–91	78	86	1.10
Cam Neely	Bos	1993–94	49	50	1.02
*Current to 1998–99					

2.26 C. 100 goals

As expected, the NHL mark for most goals in a regular season and postseason belongs to Wayne Gretzky. But No. 99 didn't tally the league's best combined season totals during 1981–82, his record-breaking 92-goal regular season. That year Gretzky scored five playoff goals in five games before his Edmonton Oilers were defeated by Los Angeles. No. 99's best goal-scoring year, including playoffs, came two years later in 1983–84 when he combined 87 regular-season goals and 13 playoff goals. Gretzky is the only player ever to crack the 100-goal plateau.

2.27 B. The Los Angeles Kings

Wayne Gretzky became the first player in NHL history to score 100 career playoff goals on May 7, 1993, during Game 3 of the divisional finals against Vancouver. Although Gretzky reached the century mark first, his accomplishment was anything but assured going into the 1993 playoffs. Shadowing Gretzky, who had 95 playoff goals, was teammate Jari Kurri, with 93 goals. Kurri notched his 100th playoff marker on May 21, just six games after Gretzky notched No. 100.

2.28 D. 24 of 122 goals

Among his 122 career playoff goals, Wayne Gretzky scored a record 24 game winners—the most in postseason play. On average the Great One decided a playoff contest he participated in every fifth goal he scored.

2.29 C. 10 scoring titles

Of the dozens of scoring records owned by Wayne Gretzky, this one may be his most impressive. No. 99 has won 10 Art Ross Trophies as the NHL's top scorer, including seven in a row during the 1980s. From 1981 to 1994, the only player to break the Great One's stranglehold on the scoring race was Mario Lemieux, who won the crown in 1988, 1989, 1992 and 1993. Lemieux also won it in 1996 and 1997.

2.30 C. 82 per cent

In 1,487 regular-season games played, Wayne Gretzky scored at least one point in every four of five games—or 82 per cent of the time. According to hockey's other great one, Detroit head coach Scotty Bowman, as quoted in *The Sporting News*, "That's like a batter hitting .400 lifetime. It's like a basketball player averaging 50 points for his entire career and a football player running for 3,000 yards a season." Lifetime, Gretzky's points-per-game average is even more remarkable: better than two points per game on average in 20 NHL seasons.

GAME 2
NO. 99'S FIRST STANLEY CUP

In this game, 25 Edmonton Oiler players and managers from Wayne Gretzky's first Stanley Cup team in 1984 appear in the puzzle horizontally, vertically or backward. Some are easily found, such as GRETZKY, others require a more careful search. After you've circled all 25 names, read the remaining 11 letters in descending order to reveal our mystery player who won the Conn Smythe Trophy as playoff MVP that season.

To help you get started, two of the words in the puzzle are: *Edmonton* and *Oilers*.

(Solutions are on page 119)

```
J   M   O   R   T   S   D   N   I   L   H   Y
A   L   I   N   S   E   M   A   N   U   U   E
C   N   M   R   E   L   K   C   U   M   G   F
K   O   D   I   R   R   U   K   N   L   H   F
S   T   N   E   A   A   R   K   O   E   E   O
O   G   M   A   R   E   Z   S   T   Y   S   C
N   N   R   N   C   S   H   U   N   T   E   R
N   I   E   E   G   H   O   G   O   O   M   R
I   L   I   E   T   R   E   N   M   P   E   E
L   K   S   R   R   Z   E   R   D   L   N   H
O   C   S   G   H   S   K   G   E   O   K   T
G   O   E   H   U   D   D   Y   G   W   O   A
O   P   M   I   F   E   O   I   L   E   R   S
F   D   N   A   L   L   E   L   C   C   M   R
```

3

THE GRETZKY FACTOR

No hockey player has inspired more quotes than Wayne Gretzky. They've come from journeymen, such as Bill Houlder, who said after his first shift against No. 99, "I didn't know whether to check him or ask for his autograph." And from Hall-of-Famers such as Gordie Howe, who concluded, "I sometimes think if you part Wayne's hair, you'll find another eye." Scoring ace Marcel Dionne once said, "There's a record book for Wayne Gretzky and one for everyone else in the league." In this chapter, we look at the impact and influence of the Gretzky factor on other players.

(Answers are on page 40)

3.1   How many *more* shorthanded playoff goals did Wayne Gretzky score in his career than Mark Messier?
A. Only one more goal
B. Two more goals
C. Three more goals
D. Gretzky doesn't have more goals; Messier does

3.2   After winning an automobile for copping the MVP award at the 1989 All-Star Game, Wayne Gretzky announced he was giving his prize to someone else. Who?
A. His father, Walter Gretzky
B. His wife, Janet
C. His agent and personal friend, Mike Barnett
D. His former teammate, Dave Semenko

3.3   What goalie assisted on the most Wayne Gretzky goals?
A. Mike Richter
B. Andy Moog
C. Grant Fuhr
D. Kelly Hrudey

3.4   Which left winger played the longest on the Edmonton
      Oilers' Wayne Gretzky–Jari Kurri line?
      A. Dave Semenko
      B. Esa Tikkanen
      C. Mike Krushelnyski
      D. Craig Simpson

3.5   Which player tied Wayne Gretzky for the scoring lead and
      prevented him from winning the scoring championship in his
      first NHL season?
      A. Marcel Dionne
      B. Gilbert Perreault
      C. Bryan Trottier
      D. Guy Lafleur

3.6   How many goals did Jari Kurri score from Wayne Gretzky
      passes during his 601-goal career?
      A. 100 to 200 goals
      B. 200 to 300 goals
      C. 300 to 400 goals
      D. 400 to 500 goals

3.7   Whose cross-check on Wayne Gretzky during the 1991
      Canada Cup caused the NHL to change its rules and assess an
      automatic game-misconduct penalty to anyone who hits
      another player from behind?
      A. The U.S.A.'s Gary Suter
      B. The Soviet Union's Viacheslav Fetisov
      C. The U.S.A.'s Chris Chelios
      D. Sweden's Ulf Samuelsson

3.8   Who owns the No. 99 jersey that Wayne Gretzky wore when
      he scored his 801st goal to tie Gordie Howe's all-time goal-
      scoring record?
      A. Wayne Gretzky's close friend and agent, Mike Barnett
      B. Wayne Gretzky's father, Walter Gretzky
      C. Wayne Gretzky himself
      D. The Hockey Hall of Fame

3.9 Which playmaker assisted on the most goals by Wayne Gretzky in his drive to reach the all-time record of 802 goals?
A. Paul Coffey
B. Mark Messier
C. Jari Kurri
D. Glenn Anderson

3.10 Which goalie was involved in two of Wayne Gretzky's five-goal games?
A. Pete Peeters
B. Don Beaupre
C. Rick Wamsley
D. Mike Liut

3.11 Who did Wayne Gretzky consider the best player in the world in 1998?
A. Dominik Hasek
B. Eric Lindros
C. Mark Messier
D. Paul Kariya

3.12 Who is Mikko Leinonen?
A. The best man at Wayne Gretzky's wedding
B. An NHLer who shares a playoff record with Wayne Gretzky
C. Finland's Wayne Gretzky, a cousin of Jari Kurri
D. The peewee goalie who gave up Wayne Gretzky's very first goal

3.13 Which Montreal Canadiens goalie predicted that Guy Lafleur would put Wayne Gretzky "in his back pocket"?
A. Patrick Roy
B. Rogatien Vachon
C. Richard Sevigny
D. Ken Dryden

3.14 Which Calgary Flames player was credited with the goal that the Edmonton Oilers' Steve Smith scored on his own net in the 1986 playoffs?
A. John Tonelli
B. Perry Berezan
C. Paul Reinhart
D. Steve Bozek

3.15 Which goalie did Wayne Gretzky beat to break Gordie Howe's NHL 801-goal record?
A. Arturs Irbe
B. Kirk McLean
C. Chris Osgood
D. Mike Vernon

3.16 Which NHL coach was criticizing Wayne Gretzky when he said: "You have to expect your best players to carry the team and that's not happening"?
A. Glen Sather
B. Larry Robinson
C. Mike Keenan
D. Barry Melrose

3.17 Whose postseason career-points record did Wayne Gretzky beat when he scored his 177th playoff point in 1987?
A. Gordie Howe
B. Jean Beliveau
C. Stan Mikita
D. Henri Richard

3.18 How many players were involved in the 1988 Edmonton–Los Angeles trade of Wayne Gretzky?
A. Four players
B. Six players
C. Eight players
D. 10 players

3.19 Which two players assisted on the goal that made Wayne Gretzky the highest point scorer in NHL history?
A. Edmonton's Jari Kurri and Esa Tikkanen
B. Los Angeles's Larry Robinson and Bernie Nicholls
C. Los Angeles's Steve Duchesne and Dave Taylor
D. New York's Brian Leetch and Adam Graves

3.20 Which goalie did Wayne Gretzky score the most playoff goals against?
A. Chico Resch
B. Mike Vernon
C. Billy Smith
D. Richard Brodeur

THE GRETZKY FACTOR
Answers

3.1 **D. Gretzky doesn't have more goals; Messier does**
Perhaps no player was influenced more profoundly by Wayne Gretzky than Mark Messier, who had mostly size on his side until he was teamed up with No. 99. Like everyone who played with the Great One, Messier couldn't help but improve. His hockey skills flourished in Edmonton as he became hockey's premier power forward of the 1980s and 1990s. He played in a record 236 playoff games and scored 109 goals, of which 14 were shorthanded. Gretzky with 208 postseason games ranks second all-time to Messier, with 11 man-disadvantage goals.

3.2 **D. His former teammate, Dave Semenko**
The 1989 All-Star Game was held in Edmonton, and Wayne Gretzky, who had been traded to Los Angeles before the start of the season, celebrated his return to Northlands Coliseum by notching a goal and two assists and nabbing MVP honors. Afterward, Gretzky surprised everyone, including the recently retired Semenko, by announcing he was giving the Dodge truck he

had won as MVP to his former Oilers teammate and on-ice protector. During his career, Gretzky won three All-Star MVP awards, and 18 vehicles.

3.3   C. Grant Fuhr

Wayne Gretzky called Grant Fuhr the best money goalie in the business. He not only shut the door on opponents but his transitional game earned him an NHL-record 14 assists in 1983–84. In his career, Gretzky scored 11 times off assists from Fuhr; Andy Moog, who ranks second in the goalie-assist category, set up four Gretzky goals.

3.4   B. Esa Tikkanen

With the exception of Philadelphia's Legion of Doom Line, few teams in the 1980s and 1990s found the right player combination to form a potent threesome. Two-man units with the third forward in rotation have become the norm. It's not because of any particular hockey philosophy, but today there are more clubs, less depth of talent on each team and fewer coaches willing to let lines develop as pressure mounts for instant success. When Wayne Gretzky and Jari Kurri teamed up in the early 1980s, their mobility and natural offensive skills became the vanguard for the Oilers' flying assault. Kurri could switch lanes in mid-attack to feed Gretzky. Gretzky, from any angle, but especially from behind the opponent's net, would set up Kurri for a one-timer or score himself on the wraparound. They knew each other's positions on the ice almost without looking. Playing together became second nature. Although many left wingers guested on their line, the most frequent one was Esa Tikkanen, who played with the duo for almost three full seasons, winning two Stanley Cups and racking up his best numbers. In 1986–87, the trio combined for 369 points.

3.5   A. Marcel Dionne

Although Wayne Gretzky tied Marcel Dionne with 137 points in the NHL scoring race in 1979–80, No. 99 lost the title because Dionne had scored more goals—53 compared to Gretzky's 51. In his autobiography *Gretzky*, Wayne asks, "What did that say to all the kids who'd heard a thousand times, 'an assist is as important as a goal'?"

3.6   C. 300 to 400 goals
In 13 NHL seasons together, hockey's greatest playmaker and one of its best scorers teamed up to put a lot of pucks in the net. The Gretzky-Kurri unit began in earnest on January 11, 1981, against the Nordiques in Quebec City when Kurri scored three times, all on assists from Gretzky. In all, the Great One helped Kurri score 364 goals and 429 total goals (combined regular season and playoffs) with Edmonton and Los Angeles—a stunning 61 per cent of Kurri's career tallies. Luc Robitaille is second in Gretzky-assisted goals with 115.

3.7   A. The U.S.A.'s Gary Suter
During Game 1 of the 1991 Canada Cup championship series, Team USA defenseman Gary Suter cross-checked Wayne Gretzky into the corner boards behind the U.S. net. Gretzky slumped to the ice in pain. Incredibly no penalty was called on the play. Although he was able to leave the ice under his own power, Gretzky was sidelined for the rest of the series with back spasms. After the incident, the Great One was dogged by chronic back pain and the condition eventually forced him to miss half of the 1992–93 season. Even though the check wasn't penalized, the NHL realized how close the hit had come to ending the career of hockey's premier player. As a result, the league began assessing automatic game misconducts to any player who hit or pushed another player from behind.

3.8   A. Wayne Gretzky's close friend and agent, Mike Barnett
Wayne Gretzky gave the 801 jersey to Mike Barnett on March 20, 1994, the night he equaled Gordie Howe's famous goal total. According to witnesses, Barnett, who hadn't owned a Gretzky game-worn sweater to that point, was speechless. As thanks, Barnett purchased the Pacific Coliseum net in which his most famous client scored his 802nd goal and gave it to the Great One for his Toronto restaurant.

3.9   C. Jari Kurri
No. 99 reached his famed 802nd career goal on 194 assists by Juri Kurri—almost 25 per cent of No. 99's goals. Of those 802

goals, Gretzky scored against 135 goalies; tallied nine goals celebrating his birthday, January 26; scored seven goals in the first minute of games and 62 goals in the final minute of play; earned goals against Mike Vernon of the Calgary Flames every year since 1986; scored against six Mikes (Vernon, Liut, Blake, Richter, Veisor and Palmateer) and three Michels (Dion, Larocque and Plasse); and tallied his quickest goal eight seconds after the opening faceoff (December 14, 1983) and six goals with one second left on the clock.

3.10 D. Mike Liut

No NHLer has recorded more five-goal games than Wayne Gretzky. In his career, the Great One potted a league-record four five-goal games. His most consistent target was Mike Liut, who twice experienced Gretzky's greatest goal-scoring sprees. The second time, on December 15, 1984, Liut was only in for No. 99's fifth goal, as Rick Wamsley bore the brunt of St. Louis's 8–2 loss. But the first time, February 18, 1981, Liut will never forget. He was still on a high from his MVP performance at the 1981 All-Star Game. "Kevin Lowe comes in on a breakaway and dekes me into the back of the net," recalled Liut, as quoted in *Sports Illustrated*. "I make the save but I'm floundering, and Gretzky scored on the rebound. I put my head down, and I'm thinking, 'It's okay, we're still in this thing.' But while my head was down, I missed the draw. I look up, and here comes Gretzky on a breakaway. He puts it right through me. Nine seconds, two Gretzky goals. I got the hook." Liut allowed three goals, and Ed Staniowski two, in Edmonton's 9–2 shellacking of the Blues.

3.11 A. Dominik Hasek

The 1997–98 season wasn't very good for Wayne Gretzky, especially against Dominik Hasek. No. 99 lost his only chance at an Olympic medal to Hasek and the Czech Republic after the Dominator whitewashed Canada's snipers in a shootout that decided the finalists for the gold-medal game. Later, on March 2, 1998, Hasek blanked the New York Rangers for the third consecutive game in a 1–0 loss. It marked the first time New York was shut out by one team three straight since Montreal did it in 1927. "I think right now he's the best player in the game," said Gretzky.

3.12 B. An NHLer who shares a playoff record with Wayne Gretzky

Among the players Wayne Gretzky shares NHL records with, no one is less famous than the New York Rangers' Mikko Leinonen, who set a playoff record with six assists in a 7–3 victory over Philadelphia on April 8, 1982. No. 99 equaled the record five years later against Los Angeles in a 13–3 bombing on April 9, 1987.

3.13 C. Richard Sevigny

Richard Sevigny's quotation came during the 1981 playoffs when Guy Lafleur and Wayne Gretzky met in their first postseason play. Lafleur, the game's most exciting player in six previous seasons, had reached his peak, while Gretzky, after a 164-point scoring binge that season, seemed poised to assume the Flower's place. In the first game, Gretzky scored a playoff-record five assists in the 6–3 win over Montreal. After the sixth goal, Gretzky skated past the Canadiens' net and patted his rear end, a jab at Sevigny and his "back-pocket" line. Gretzky dominated the best-of-five series, playing in a different class from even Lafleur. The Oilers swept Montreal three games straight.

3.14 B. Perry Berezan

It was the seventh game of the Edmonton-Calgary divisional finals. With the score tied early in the third period, Flames forward Perry Berezan dumped the puck into the Oilers' zone and headed to the Calgary bench for a line change. Rookie Steve Smith, being chased by Lanny McDonald, skated behind his own net and launched the puck toward teammate Glenn Anderson. But the cross-ice pass banked off the leg of Oilers goalie Grant Fuhr, parked at the edge of the crease, and slid into the Edmonton net. Berezan, the last Flame to touch the puck, was credited with the goal—one he didn't even see go in. Smith, who was celebrating his 23rd birthday, fell to the ice in shame and utter disbelief. Calgary held the lead and scuttled the Oilers' dream of a dynasty and a third straight Stanley Cup.

Wayne Gretzky, the consummate team player, remembered Smith's anguish the following year (1987) after Edmonton won its third Cup. The first player Gretzky handed the trophy to for the ceremonial skate around the rink was Smith.

3.15 B. Kirk McLean
Wayne Gretzky tied Gordie Howe with No. 801 on goalie Arturs Irbe on March 20, 1994. Three nights later, on March 23, he shattered Howe's career goal-scoring record, potting his 802nd on a second-period power-play goal against the Vancouver Canucks' Kirk McLean. The Great One needed only 1,117 games to eclipse Howe's mark. Howe took 1,767 matches—or about eight seasons *more* than Gretzky.

3.16 C. Mike Keenan
During the 1996 Detroit–St. Louis Western Conference semifinals, Mike Keenan publicly questioned Wayne Gretzky's performance, saying, among other things, "If he's not injured, then something must be bothering him." Keenan also berated the Great One in front of his teammates, which prompted Oilers general manager Glen Sather to muse: "I think [Keenan] should have his head examined. As far as I'm concerned, he must be touched by the wind or something to be critical of a guy like Wayne Gretzky." Later, Keenan apologized to No. 99, saying he might have "overstepped" himself in his comments.

3.17 B. Jean Beliveau
When Wayne Gretzky recorded his 177th playoff point on a Jari Kurri goal on April 9, 1987, he broke the 16-year-old 176-point record of Jean Beliveau. It was the Great One's 82nd playoff game; Big Jean took 162 games.

3.18 C. Eight players
On August 9, 1988, Edmonton Oilers owner Peter Pocklington became the most hated man in the city after trading away Wayne Gretzky to Los Angeles with Marty McSorley and Mike Krushelnyski for the Kings' Jimmy Carson, Martin Gelinas, three first-round drafts and $15 million in cash. The picks

were: Jason Miller in 1989, Martin Rucinsky in 1991 and Nick Stajduhar in 1993. Including Gretzky, eight players exchanged jerseys. Some people blamed No. 99's new wife, Janet Jones, for his move to L.A. But it was mostly about money and Pocklington's failure at other business ventures. To prove that point, if it wasn't about cash, why was the deal made at the ownership level rather than in the conventional manner between general managers? Pocklington still lives in Edmonton.

3.19 C. Los Angeles's Steve Duchesne and Dave Taylor
Gordie Howe's career total of 1,850 points was considered unassailable until Wayne Gretzky entered the NHL and began destroying all existing scoring records. Fittingly, on October 15, 1989, Howe's number fell in Edmonton, the city where Gretzky rose to prominence. Historic point No. 1,851 came on a game-tying goal with 53 seconds left in regulation time. The setup men were Gretzky's L.A. teammates Steve Duchesne and Dave Taylor. Rather than playing in his "office," behind the opponent's net, Gretzky positioned himself in front of Bill Ranford. Duchesne's pass hopped over a stick, bounced off Taylor's knee and came right to Gretzky, who backhanded it over a sprawling Ranford. The game was halted as Howe came out to take part in ceremonies honoring the NHL's new point king. Interestingly the first time Howe met Gretzky, when he was just a boy, it was Howe's advice to practice backhand shots. Gretzky scored many backhanders, including his first WHA goal, his first NHL goal and the goal that broke Howe's record, point No. 1,851.

3.20 B. Mike Vernon
Wayne Gretzky put 12 playoff pucks past Vernon, the most frequent postseason casualty of No. 99. Another backstopping target was Chico Resch, who said of Gretzky in *Sports Illustrated*: "What I want to know is, how did he always know what the toughest play would be for a goalie to make? He was always jamming me on my glove side, shoulder high, or putting the puck eight or 10 inches off the ice on my stick side. With Wayne there was no routine plays. Was he a goaltender once? Did Walter [Gretzky, Wayne's father,] teach him that?"

GAME 3
MILESTONE TARGETS

The Great One scored his milestone goals against a variety of opponents. Who allowed Wayne Gretzky's first NHL goal, or his record-breaking 802nd? Unscramble the goalies or team names by placing each letter in the correct order in the boxes. Then unscramble the letters in the circled boxes to spell out the four-word phrase that describes how Gretzky scored his 500th NHL goal.

(Solutions are on page 120)

NNALOH

SREETEP

U L T I

URROBED

S E L F R Y

ORNAFRD

LAMNEC

SLO SNAGLEE

49

4

TRUE OR FALSE?

Wayne Gretzky was nicknamed the Great One at age nine. True or False? In this chapter, we pick up the pace with a series of right-or-wrong questions that give you a 50-50 chance of scoring a trivia point. When did Gretzky really become the Great One? Some accounts say as early as age nine or 10 when he scored 378 goals in 68 games in novice hockey. Later, in Grade 8 at Greenbrier School in Brantford, some people recall that "Great Gretzky" was on the walls and posters of the school. But it wasn't until Gretzky was 16 and playing junior hockey in the Ontario Hockey Assocation that the Great Gretzky, which eventually became the Great One, first stuck in the public's consciousness. Singled out for his talents since he was six years old, Gretzky finally received the most difficult of nicknames—the Great One.

(Answers are on page 53)

4.1 On the day Wayne Gretzky was born, his hockey hero, Gordie Howe, scored an NHL goal. *True or False?*

4.2 Wayne Gretzky is the only NHLer to wear No. 99 on an NHL hockey sweater. *True or False?*

4.3 In 1987–88, the year Wayne Gretzky was traded to Los Angeles, the Edmonton Oilers allowed 99 goals with him on the ice. *True or False?*

4.4 Mark Messier scored 99 points for New York in 1995–96, the year before Wayne Gretzky came to the Rangers from St. Louis. *True or False?*

4.5 Wayne Gretzky is the only player in NHL history to win the Hart Trophy as league MVP with two different teams. *True or False?*

4.6 Bobby Orr's 1966–67 Topps rookie card is the most valuable regular-issue hockey card produced since 1950. *True or False?*

4.7 The first NHL penalty in Edmonton Oilers franchise history was assessed to Wayne Gretzky. *True or False?*

4.8 Wayne Gretzky scored his first 50th goal the same night Guy Lafleur scored his last 50th. *True or False?*

4.9 Believe it or not, Paul Coffey assisted on the most goals of both Wayne Gretzky and Mario Lemieux. *True or False?*

4.10 Wayne Gretzky led his team in scoring every season throughout his entire 20-year NHL career. *True or False?*

4.11 Wayne Gretzky always tucked in his sweater on the right side. *True or False?*

4.12 None of Wayne Gretzky's brothers ever played in the NHL. *True or False?*

4.13 Wayne Gretzky was the last remaining NHLer who once played in the World Hockey Association. *True or False?*

4.14 Wayne Gretzky notched his first and last career points on goals by defensemen. *True or False?*

4.15 Wayne Gretzky is the only NHLer to win a league MVP award more than six times. *True or False?*

4.16 The only player with more scoring championships than Gordie Howe is Wayne Gretzky. *True or False?*

4.17 Wayne Gretzky scored his 2,000th career point and 700th career goal in the same season, 1990–91. *True or False?*

4.18 Wayne Gretzky and Bobby Hull are the only players to score 50 goals in one season in the WHA and the NHL. *True or False?*

4.19 Wayne Gretzky scored his first NHL goal in his third NHL game. *True or False?*

4.20 The highest-rated regular-season game on CBC's *Hockey Night in Canada* was the last NHL game Wayne Gretzky played on April 18, 1999. *True or False?*

4.21 Wayne Gretzky led Edmonton in goal scoring every year he was with the Oilers. *True or False?*

4.22 Despite all the awards and accolades over the years, Wayne Gretzky never received the prestigious *Sports Illustrated* Sportsman of the Year Award. *True or False?*

4.23 Wayne Gretzky is the only NHLer to win a major individual award in five or more consecutive seasons. *True or False?*

4.24 Wayne Gretzky scored more points after his trade to Los Angeles than all five players/draft picks Edmonton received. *True or False?*

4.25 Wayne Gretzky scored his 2,500th point in fewer than 1,000 games. *True or False?*

4.26 Wayne Gretzky was runner-up to Mike Gartner as WHA Rookie of the Year in 1979. *True or False?*

4.27 Wayne Gretzky scored more assists than the six Sutter brothers combined. *True or False?*

4.28 Wayne Gretzky met his future wife, Janet Jones, at the 1981 All-Star Game in Los Angeles. *True or False?*

4.29 Wayne Gretzky averaged more NHL points per game in Canada than in U.S. appearances. *True or False?*

4.30 Wayne Gretzky and Mario Lemieux never met in a Stanley Cup playoff game. *True or False?*

4.31 Tony Esposito was the only netminder in history to surrender goals to both Gordie Howe and Wayne Gretzky. *True or False?*

4.32 Despite his scoring feats, Wayne Gretzky doesn't hold the NHL record for most career hat tricks. *True or False?*

4.33 Wayne Gretzky has more assists than any other NHLer has points. *True or False?*

4.34 Wayne Gretzky is the only NHLer to win two MVP awards— the Hart Trophy as MVP in the regular season and the Conn Smythe Trophy as playoff MVP—in the same year. *True or False?*

4.35 Wayne Gretzky only scored one playoff overtime goal in his career. *True or False?*

4.36 Wayne Gretzky was *not* the first player selected in 1977's Junior A draft. *True or False?*

4.37 Wayne Gretzky is the only player ever to win NHL scoring titles with two different teams. *True or False?*

4.38 Wayne Gretzky's nickname with the WHA Indianapolis Racers was Brinks. *True or False?*

4.39 Wayne Gretzky is the first player to have his uniform number retired by the NHL. *True or False?*

TRUE OR FALSE?
Answers

4.1 True
On January 26, 1961, Wayne Gretzky's birth date, Gordie Howe scored his 467th NHL goal. Eighteen years later, when No. 99 entered the NHL, Howe's goal lead stood at 786–0, with

a comfortable 1,809–0 in points. In 11 seasons, Gretzky would smash Howe's all-time NHL point total of 1,850, and in 15 seasons, his league goal aggregate of 801.

4.2 False

Wayne Gretzky's famous No. 99 wasn't the only double-digit nines in NHL history. In fact, almost a half century before Gretzky, in 1934–35, three different Montreal Canadiens players donned 99s, none making any obvious impact. In modern times, a few other 99s sprouted up around the league, perhaps in the hope of capturing the Gretzky magic. Toronto's Wilf Paiement, who entered the NHL the same season as Gretzky, 1979–80, wore his No. 99 for three years with the Maple Leafs. Soon after, Winnipeg boasted Rick Dudley in a Jets No. 99 uniform. "I went to Edmonton for a game and the fans gave me such a hard time," Dudley said, as quoted in a *National Post* story. "I said, 'Maybe they are right. Maybe I should not wear this number.' I took it off." First overall draft pick Brian Lawton, wanting some of the magic without too much of the comparison, chose No. 98 in his 1983–84 rookie season with Minnesota.

4.3 True

In Wayne Gretzky's last season in Edmonton, the Great One had a TGA (team goals against) of 99, the lowest goals-against total in his nine-year stint with the Oilers.

4.4 True

Mark Messier only scored 99 points (47 goals, 52 assists) once in his 20-plus-year career—in New York in 1995–96. Wayne Gretzky joined Messier and the Rangers the following season.

4.5 False

While Wayne Gretzky won MVP status on multiple occasions with Edmonton (eight times) and once in Los Angeles, he isn't the only NHLer so distinguished. Mark Messier's two Hart Trophies were split between Edmonton (1990) and New York (1992).

4.6 False

Bobby Orr's Topps rookie card from 1966–67 is valued at $2,500 U.S. in mint condition, but it still ranks second in dollar value to Gordie Howe's 1951–52 Parkhurst card, which is listed at $3,000 U.S., as is Bobby Hull's rookie card from 1957–58. Wayne Gretzky's 1979–80 O-Pee-Chee rookie card is listed at $900 U.S.

4.7 True

At 5:19 of the first period in Edmonton's first NHL game on October 10, 1979, Wayne Gretzky took the Oilers' first penalty in history, receiving two minutes for slashing.

4.8 True

The torch was truly passed from one superstar in one era of hockey to the next generation's superstar on April 2, 1980, when Guy Lafleur and Wayne Gretzky each scored 50th goals. It was the sixth and final time Lafleur would score a 50th marker and the first of nine for the Great One. Amazingly the goalie who gave up Gretzky's first 50th, Gary Edwards, was the same netminder Lafleur scored his very first NHL goal against.

4.9 False

Fantastic, if it were true, but it's not; it's only very close to the truth. No player helped Mario Lemieux score more than Paul Coffey did. He assisted on 72 of Lemieux's 613 regular-season goals with the Pittsburgh Penguins. In Edmonton, Coffey fed the Great One 116 times for goals, second only to Jari Kurri with 194 helpers.

4.10 False

The only season Wayne Gretzky failed to lead his club in scoring was 1992–93 when he was diagnosed with a herniated thoracic disc. He missed the first 39 games (the most in any season), scored an incredible 65 points in the next 45 matches and surrendered Los Angeles's scoring lead to Luc Robitaille (125 points). In that season, Gretzky came the closest to winning another Stanley Cup after his Edmonton days, amassing a playoff-high 40 points in 24 games before bowing to Montreal in the Cup finals.

4.11 True

Wayne Gretzky never changed the sweater tuck his father first tried when Wayne was just six years old. In his Edmonton days, Nike supplied the Oilers with their jerseys in exchange for having the Nike logo on the lower right side of the sweater. But Gretzky's tuck-in hid the logo. After some discussion, Nike sent over a new set of uniforms. The logo was now on the left side.

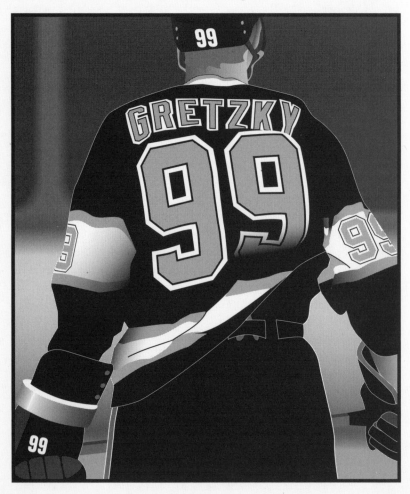

4.12 False

Like a number of siblings of superstars (such as those of Mario Lemieux, Marcel Dionne and Gordie Howe), Wayne's younger brother, Brent, had a brief career. He played 13 games for Tampa Bay in 1993–94 and 1994–95, netting one goal and three assists for four points.

4.13 False

There were only three former World Hockey Association players still active in the NHL in 1997–98: Mark Messier, Mike Gartner and Wayne Gretzky. Each one has had a distinguished hockey career, and they all played one WHA season in 1978–79. Gretzky was the top scorer of the trio, notching 110 points in a season split between Indianapolis and Edmonton. Messier played in Indianapolis and Cincinnati and Gartner in Cincinnati. Messier is the last former WHA player still active, after the retirement of Gartner in 1998 and Gretzky in 1999.

4.14 True

Hockey's best playmaker made everyone play better, including defensemen such as Kevin Lowe and Brian Leetch, who each scored goals on Wayne Gretzky's first and last career points. Gretzky bookended his career with point No. 1 off Lowe's goal on October 10, 1979, against Chicago, while point No. 2,857 resulted from Leetch's marker on April 19, 1999, against Pittsburgh. Gretzky picked up his first point in the first period of his first NHL game; his last point also came in the first period. Trivial but true, both defensemen's family names begin with *L*.

4.15 True

In his prime, Wayne Gretzky completely dominated the NHL awards, winning the Hart Trophy as league MVP an unparalleled nine times, eight titles consecutively between 1980 and 1987. In one year, 1985, Gretzky was a double MVP winner, also earning the Conn Smythe Trophy as playoff MVP. Gordie Howe is the only other NHLer with six Hart Trophies. In fact, only Gretzky, Howe and Kareem Abdul-Jabbar have won as many as six league MVP awards in North American pro sports.

4.16 True

Gordie Howe won the Art Ross Trophy as the league's leading scorer six times, including four in a row between 1950 and 1954, another in 1956–57 and his last in his 17th NHL season (1962–63). The only other NHLer with more scoring championships than Howe's six-pack (and the six titles won by Mario Lemieux) is Wayne Gretzky, who owns 10 Art Ross Trophies.

4.17 True

In 1990–91, Wayne Gretzky scored his 2,000th point (October 26, 1990) and his 700th career goal (January 3, 1991) en route to his ninth scoring title in 11 years. He finished the season with 163 points. Gretzky was the first NHLer to reach the 2,000-point mark and the fourth to hit the 700-goal mark.

4.18 False

Only two players notched 50-goal seasons in both the WHA and the NHL, but Wayne Gretzky wasn't one of them. In his only WHA year, he netted 46 goals, compared to his nine 50-goal seasons in the NHL. Bobby Hull had five 50-goal years in the NHL before recording another four in the WHA (to equal Gretzky's career total of nine). So who was the only other sniper to notch 50 in a season in both pro leagues? Originally with Pittsburgh and Toronto, Blaine Stoughton blossomed in the WHA, scoring 52 goals with Cincinnati in 1976–77. Later, after the NHL-WHA merger in 1979, he returned to the NHL to notch two 50-plus-goal seasons—56 goals to share the goal-scoring lead in 1979–80 and 52 goals (the sixth-best total) in 1981–82. Stoughton is still Carolina-Hartford's only 50-goal man.

4.19 True

No. 99 scored goal No. 1 in his third NHL game on October 14, 1979, against the Vancouver Canucks' Glen Hanlon. Hanlon, incidentally, also figures in Wayne Gretzky's historic 802nd goal, 15 years later. In 1994 he was the goalie coach for the Canucks, the team Gretzky scored on to move ahead of Gordie Howe as the NHL's all-time goal-scoring leader.

4.20 True

Wayne Gretzky's final NHL game between New York and Pittsburgh drew an average audience of 2,161,000 viewers with a peak of 2,811,000 between 6:00 and 6:30 p.m. ET. Those numbers represent the highest ever for a regular-season game on *Hockey Night in Canada.*

4.21 False

Wayne Gretzky was topped twice by his Edmonton Oilers teammates in the club's goal-scoring derby. In 1985–86, Jari Kurri (68) and Glenn Anderson (54) scored more goals than Gretzky (52). Then Craig Simpson (56) and Jari Kurri (43) both outscored Gretzky (40) in 1987–88, his last Oilers season.

4.22 False

Since it was founded in 1954, *Sports Illustrated* has honored three hockey players/teams with Sportsman of the Year Awards: Bobby Orr (1970), the gold-medal U.S. Olympic team (1980) and Wayne Gretzky (1982).

4.23 False

Although Wayne Gretzky won seven straight Art Ross Trophies as scoring leader and eight consecutive Hart Trophies as league MVP, two other players had continuous award-winning seasons to equal or almost equal Gretzky. Jacques Plante won five straight Vezina Trophies as top netminder (1956 to 1960) and Bobby Orr took the Norris Trophy as best defenseman eight times between 1968 and 1975.

4.24 True

From the start of 1988–89 through to the end of 1998–99, Wayne Gretzky outscored the combined total of the five players he was traded for: Jimmy Carson, Martin Gelinas, Jason Miller, Martin Rucinsky and Nick Stajduhar. No. 99 had 1,118 points in 791 games, compared to the combined sum of 1,040 points in 1,599 games amassed by the five. At the time of Gretzky's retirement, only Gelinas and Rucinsky were still in the NHL.

4.25 False

Wayne Gretzky reached the 2,500-point plateau on a Rob Blake goal on April 17, 1995. It was his 1,165th game.

4.26 False

In fact, Mike Gartner, who played his rookie season in Cincinnati with the WHA Stingers, was Wayne Gretzky's runner-up as WHA Rookie of the Year in 1979. In the WHA scoring race, Gretzky finished third (behind Real Cloutier and Robbie Ftorek) with a 46–64–110 record, while Gartner managed 27–25–52.

4.27 True

Brent, Brian, Darryl, Duane, Rich and Ron Sutter have a combined 1,607 assists in 4,895 games, compared to Wayne Gretzky's 1,963 assists in 1,487 games.

4.28 False

Wayne Gretzky and Janet Jones first met during the early 1980s on the TV show *Dance Fever*. Gretzky was a celebrity judge, Janet a dancer. They married in 1988; both were 27 years old. Janet has starred in *The Flamingo Kid*, *Police Academy 5* and *A League of Their Own*.

4.29 True

Wayne Gretzky played better in Canadian cities, with a 2.2 career points-per-game average, compared to games in the United States, where he averaged 1.7 points per game. This significant difference of .5 points per game is due partly to the fact that the Great One's best scoring years were with Edmonton, the city where he played half his games for nine seasons. During that time, he scored 1,669 points, or more than 58 per cent of his total career points. Overall, Gretzky scored 2,857 career points in 1,487 games for a 1.9 points-per-game average.

4.30 True

The NHL's two greatest modern-day scorers never opposed each other in a playoff game. The best chance of a postseason meeting was 1993 when Wayne Gretzky led the Los Angeles

Kings to the finals. But Mario Lemieux's Pittsburgh Penguins, the top overall regular-season team, were upset by the New York Islanders in the Patrick Division finals.

4.31 False

In fact, eight goaltenders have been scored upon by Wayne Gretzky and Gordie Howe: Tony Esposito, Robbie Holland, Mike Liut, Mario Lessard, Markus Mattsson, Greg Millen, Mike Palmateer and Rogatien Vachon.

4.32 False

In 20 seasons, Wayne Gretzky scored a record 50 hat tricks. He had 37 three-goal games, nine four-goal games and four five-goal games. The next closest rival is Mike Bossy with 39 hat tricks.

4.33 True

If you take away all of Wayne Gretzky's 894 goals, he still out-points every player in NHL history with 1,963 assists, 113 more points than Gordie Howe's 1,850 career points. The momentous point came on October 26, 1997, when the Great One notched his 1,850th and 1,851th assists of his career. The assist that broke Howe's all-time mark was classic Gretzky. He fed New York Rangers teammate Niklas Sundstrom in the right circle, then came in behind Sundstrom for a return pass. Gretzky waited briefly, allowing Ulf Samuelsson to join the play late. When Samuelsson skated into the slot, Gretzky pinpointed a perfect tape-to-tape pass in front, and Samuelsson slammed it past Anaheim's Guy Herbert. A long standing ovation followed as Madison Square Garden fans chanted, "Gretzky, Gretzky!"

4.34 False

While Wayne Gretzky won the NHL's two MVP trophies in one year, 1985, two other players did it before him: Guy Lafleur in 1977 and Bobby Orr in 1970 and 1972.

4.35 False

Wayne Gretzky played in 208 playoff matches of a potential 211, scored a league-leading 122 playoff goals and netted four postseason overtime goals. All told, he played in 39 overtime playoff games.

4.36 False

Despite off-the-chart numbers in scoring in minor hockey and Junior B, Wayne Gretzky was actually selected third in the 1977 Ontario Junior A draft. The Oshawa Generals, who picked first, chose Tom McCarthy; the Kitchener Rangers, with the second pick, took Paul Reinhart. The Sault Ste. Marie Greyhounds, who drafted third, chose the 17-year-old Gretzky, who lit up the OHA in his rookie season, scoring 182 points in 64 games. Why wasn't Gretzky drafted first? The Peterborough Petes, who drew fourth pick, wanted Gretzky badly and made deals with Oshawa and Kitchener. But they didn't work anything out with the Greyhounds. So Sault Ste. Marie got Gretzky, and despite protests by Walter Gretzky concerning the distance from Brantford (500 miles), Wayne played his only full OHA season in the Soo.

4.37 False

To put Wayne Gretzky's monster trade to Los Angeles in perspective, no NHL scoring champion in modern times has ever been dealt at the height of his career and repeated as scoring champion with a second team. Gretzky led the league seven times in Edmonton and three times in Los Angeles. Before that, only one other NHLer had done it—the legendary Joe Malone of the Montreal Canadiens. In 1917–18, the NHL's first season, Malone potted 44 goals in the 22-game schedule as the league's first scoring leader. Two years later he repeated as league title holder with the Quebec Bulldogs, recording 39 goals in 24 matches.

4.38 True

Wayne Gretzky's first shift as a pro came in an exhibition game between the Indianapolis Racers and the St. Louis Blues. At one point, Gretzky was challenged by Blues defenseman Barry Gibbs. Racers rearguard Kevin Nugent stepped in to defend the team's budding star. "I don't want [Gibbs] messin' with Brinks," Nugent said. "That's what we call Wayne. He has all the dough." Gretzky earned an assist in the 4–1 win.

4.39 True

After Wayne Gretzky's retirement in April 1999, the NHL announced that no player in the league will ever again wear No. 99, not that anyone in his right mind would ever consider it. The only other athlete whose number has been retired by his team, as well as by the entire sport, is baseball's Jackie Robinson. It's expected (at the time of this writing) that Gretzky will become the first player to have his number retired by three NHL teams—Edmonton, Los Angeles and the New York Rangers. St. Louis, for which Gretzky played less than a half season, will likely pass on the idea. In June 1999, Gretzky became the 10th player to have the mandatory three-year waiting period for induction waived by the Hockey Hall of Fame.

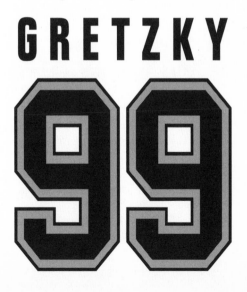

GAME 4
OTHER CLAIMS TO FAME

After Wayne Gretzky was traded to Los Angeles in August 1988, one of the jokes in Edmonton went: How cold will it be in Edmonton this winter? Minus-99. In this game, match the year in the left column with some of the most unusual aspects of Gretzky's career on and off the ice.

(Solutions are on page 120)

1. ____ 1971   A. Gretzky proposes to Janet Jones

2. ____ 1981   B. Gretzky appears on *Saturday Night Live*

3. ____ 1982   C. Gretzky is awarded the Order of Canada

4. ____ 1983   D. Andy Warhol paints Gretzky's portrait

5. ____ 1984   E. First major newspaper feature on Gretzky appears in Toronto's *Telegram*

6. ____ 1988   F. An eight-foot-high statue of Gretzky is unveiled at Northlands Coliseum in Edmonton

7. ____ 1989   G. Gretzky enlists a group of all-star friends to play in Europe during the NHL work stoppage

8. ____ 1989   H. First Gretzky-inspired book hits the market: *Gretzky*

9. ____ 1994   I. Mattel introduces a Gretzky action figure

10. ____ 1998   J. U.S. President Ronald Reagan jokes he would trade two draft choices and the state of Texas for Gretzky

5

MARIO & CO.
(THE SECOND-BESTS)

If Wayne Gretzky hadn't played hockey, Brett Hull would hold the single-season record for goals scored (86). And Mario Lemieux would own the single-season record for points scored (199). But Gretzky did play hockey and established more milestones than anyone imagined a player could. His accomplishments are staggering, especially considering the company of superstars he supersedes. In this chapter, we look at the Lemieuxs and Hulls, hockey's second-best to the Great One.

(Answers are on page 70)

5.1 **What was the greatest difference in points between Wayne Gretzky and the runner-up in an NHL scoring race?**
A. 69 points
B. 79 points
C. 89 points
D. 99 points

5.2 **How many more games did Mario Lemieux take to score 600 goals than Wayne Gretzky?**
A. Lemieux scored his 600th faster than Gretzky
B. One game
C. 66 games
D. 99 games

5.3 **Besides Wayne Gretzky, who is the only other teenager to register a 50-goal season?**
A. Pierre Larouche
B. Mario Lemieux
C. Jimmy Carson
D. Dale Hawerchuk

5.4 After Wayne Gretzky, who was the NHL's point leader in the 1980s?
A. Jari Kurri
B. Peter Stastny
C. Denis Savard
D. Paul Coffey

5.5 After Wayne Gretzky, which player recorded the most points in his first four years in the NHL?
A. Mike Bossy
B. Peter Stastny
C. Howie Morenz
D. Mario Lemieux

5.6 *The Hockey News'* 1998 poll of the top 50 players ranked Wayne Gretzky the NHL's No. 1 player of all time. Who finished second?
A. Maurice Richard
B. Bobby Orr
C. Mario Lemieux
D. Gordie Howe

5.7 After Wayne Gretzky and Mike Bossy, which player scored the most goals in his first three NHL seasons?
A. Mario Lemieux
B. Brett Hull
C. Pavel Bure
D. Joe Nieuwendyk

5.8 The first NHL sharpshooter to notch 70 goals in a season was Phil Esposito; the second was Wayne Gretzky. Who was the third player to reach the 70-goal plateau?
A. Edmonton's Jari Kurri
B. The New York Islanders' Mike Bossy
C. Pittsburgh's Mario Lemieux
D. Los Angeles's Bernie Nicholls

5.9 After Wayne Gretzky, which NHLer is the next fastest 200-goal scorer?
A. Mike Bossy
B. Eric Lindros
C. Mario Lemieux
D. Brett Hull

5.10 Who shares the record with Wayne Gretzky for the most 50-goal seasons?
A. Bobby Hull
B. Guy Lafleur
C. Phil Esposito
D. Mike Bossy

5.11 After Wayne Gretzky, who has scored the most game-winning playoff goals in his career?
A. Maurice Richard
B. Claude Lemieux
C. Mike Bossy
D. Mario Lemieux

5.12 When Wayne Gretzky scored seven assists on February 15, 1980, he tied an NHL record first set in what decade?
A. The 1940s
B. The 1950s
C. The 1960s
D. The 1970s

5.13 After Wayne Gretzky, who holds the next longest consecutive point-scoring streak in NHL history?
A. Mats Sundin
B. Guy Lafleur
C. Mario Lemieux
D. Steve Yzerman

5.14 After Wayne Gretzky, who is the next youngest MVP in NHL history?
A. Bobby Orr
B. Bryan Trottier
C. Mario Lemieux
D. Eric Lindros

5.15 Besides Wayne Gretzky, how many other NHLers have topped the 100-playoff-goal mark?
A. One player, Jari Kurri
B. Two players
C. Three players
D. Four players

5.16 After Wayne Gretzky, who scored the most assists in Stanley Cup finals action?
A. Gordie Howe and Jean Beliveau
B. Jean Beliveau and Frank Mahovlich
C. Frank Mahovlich and Jari Kurri
D. Jari Kurri and Gordie Howe

5.17 Who is the youngest NHLer to score 1,000 points, besides Wayne Gretzky and Mario Lemieux?
A. Mike Bossy
B. Guy Lafleur
C. Steve Yzerman
D. Dale Hawerchuk

5.18 In what game did Mario Lemieux notch his 500th goal?
A. His 505th game
B. His 555th game
C. His 605th game
D. His 655th game

5.19 Besides Wayne Gretzky, who was the only other player to score 200 goals for two different NHL teams?
A. Norm Ullman in Detroit and Toronto
B. Frank Mahovlich in Toronto and Montreal
C. Phil Esposito in Boston and New York
D. Lanny McDonald in Toronto and Calgary

5.20 When you compare the number of career goals scored by Mario Lemieux in his 745 career games and Wayne Gretzky's goal count after 745 games, which statement is correct?
A. Gretzky scored three more goals
B. Gretzky scored 30 more goals
C. Lemieux scored three more goals
D. Lemieux scored 30 more goals

5.21 If Guy Lafleur scored 1,000 points in 720 games, how many games did it take Wayne Gretzky to reach that notable milestone?
A. Between 300 and 400 games
B. Between 400 and 500 games
C. Between 500 and 600 games
D. Between 600 and 700 games

5.22 Wayne Gretzky's 47-point playoff total in 1985 is an NHL record. How many fewer points does Mario Lemieux have with the next-best league record?
A. One point less (46 points)
B. Three points less (44 points)
C. Five points less (42 points)
D. Seven points less (40 points)

5.23 As of 1998–99, how many playoff points does Wayne Gretzky have in 16 years of postseason action?
A. Between 250 and 300 points
B. Between 300 and 350 points
C. Between 350 and 400 points
D. More than 400 points

5.24 Besides Wayne Gretzky, how many other NHLers have scored 50 goals in fewer than 50 games?
A. Three players
B. Four players
C. Five players
D. Six players

5.25 How many other NHLers had scored 50 goals in 50 games before Wayne Gretzky did it in 1981–82?
A. Wayne Gretzky was the first
B. Only one, Maurice Richard
C. Only one, Gordie Howe
D. Two players

5.26 After Wayne Gretzky, which player scored the most points during the 1990s?
A. Brett Hull
B. Joe Sakic
C. Adam Oates
D. Steve Yzerman

MARIO & CO. (THE SECOND-BESTS)
Answers

5.1 **B. 79 points**
Between 1981–82 and 1986–87, Wayne Gretzky scored an average of 73 more points per season than his nearest rival in the scoring race. In his best year, 1983–84, No. 99 topped teammate and runner-up Paul Coffey by a staggering 79 points. Gretzky could have quit playing on January 7 and *still* captured the scoring championship—a full three months before the end of the season.

5.2 **B. One game**
The crowd chanted "Mar-i-o, Mar-i-o, Mar-i-o" and threw hundreds of hats onto the ice as Lemieux acknowledged the standing ovation with a wave of his stick. Lemieux, before a

hometown Pittsburgh crowd, had scored his 600th career goal. The historic marker, an empty-netter, came in the last minute of play against Vancouver in the Penguins' 6–4 win on February 4, 1997. It was Mario's 719th game, only one more game than it took Gretzky to score his 600th (which happened on November 23, 1988).

5.3 C. Jimmy Carson

Among the hot young snipers who have made their first NHL marks early in their careers, only Jimmy Carson has equaled Wayne Gretzky by turning in a 50-goal season before his 20th birthday. Gretzky was 19.2 when he passed the 50-goal mark in the 78th game of his first NHL season on April 2, 1980. Carson, at 19.8 years, was just six months older when he netted his 50th in the 77th game of his second season on March 26, 1988. Gretzky totaled 51 goals and Carson achieved 55 in those seasons.

The NHL's Youngest 50-Goal Scorers*

Player	Team	Date of 50th Goal	Player's Game No.	Age
Wayne Gretzky	Edm	02/04/80	78	19.2
Jimmy Carson	LA	26/03/88	77	19.8
Pierre Larouche	Pit	03/04/76	75	20.5
Craig Simpson	Edm	15/03/88	71	21.1
Mike Bossy	NYI	01/04/78	69	21.2
Mark Messier	Edm	31/03/82	78	21.3

Current to 1998–99

5.4 B. Peter Stastny

No one came remotely close to Wayne Gretzky in point-scoring totals during the 1980s. In 10 seasons between 1979–80 and 1988–89, Gretzky amassed 1,837 points. Peter Stastny had the next best NHL numbers with 1,059 points—an incredible 778 points behind the Great One. The huge point differential between Gretzky and Stastny and the rest of the league indicated the scoring prowess of No. 99 during his first decade of

NHL hockey. And Stastny was no slouch at racking up the points. As a Quebec Nordique, he became one of the league's most consistent point producers, recording 100-plus points in seven of his first eight seasons, a distinction he shares with only two other players, Gretzky and Mario Lemieux. Stastny, a Czechoslovakian defector, won the 1981 Calder Trophy as top NHL rookie.

The Top Point Scorers in the 1980s

Player	Team	Goals	Assists	Points
Wayne Gretzky	Edm/LA	626	1,216	1,842
Peter Stastny	Que	385	674	1,059
Jari Kurri	Edm	474	569	1,043
Denis Savard	Chi	351	662	1,013
Paul Coffey	Edm/Pit	283	669	952

5.5 D. Mario Lemieux

After Wayne Gretzky, who amassed the single greatest volume of points in his first four years with 709 points in 319 games, Mario Lemieux scored the next highest number with 516 points.

The NHL's Best Four-Year Starts*

Player	Team	1st	2nd	3rd	4th	Total Points
Wayne Gretzky	Edm	137	164	212	196	709
Mario Lemieux	Pit	100	141	107	168	516
Peter Stastny	Que	109	139	124	119	491
Mike Bossy	NYI	91	126	92	119	428
Dale Hawerchuk	Wpg	103	91	102	130	426

Current to 1998–99

5.6 B. Bobby Orr

To celebrate its 50th anniversary of publishing in 1998, *The Hockey News* polled 50 hockey experts to determine the NHL's top 50 players of all time. Wayne Gretzky finished first with 2,726 voter points, followed closely by Bobby Orr (2,713 points). While Orr finished just 13 points behind Gretzky,

Gordie Howe was only 32 points behind Orr with 2,681. Mario Lemieux was fourth with 2,308 points and Maurice Richard was fifth with 2,142 points.

5.7 C. Pavel Bure

The Russian Rocket blasted off into the NHL stratosphere of records, becoming the third-highest goal scorer in his first three seasons by notching 34, 60 and 60 goals between 1991 and 1994. On his dazzling flight path to 154 goals, Bure earned the 1992 Calder Trophy (top rookie), "human highlight reel" credentials as goal-scoring leader of 1993–94 and a new six-year contract with the Vancouver Canucks worth $25 million U.S. Not too shabby, considering he began his career as a sixth-round (113th overall) pick in the 1989 Entry Draft.

The NHL's Three-Year Goal-Scoring Wonders*

Player	Years	Total Games	Seasons 1st	2nd	3rd	Total Goals
W. Gretzky	1979–82	239	51	55	92	198
M. Bossy	1977–80	228	53	69	51	173
P. Bure	1991–94	224	34	60	60	154
J. Nieuwendyk	1987–90	231	51	51	45	147
M. Lemieux	1984–87	215	43	48	54	145
B. Hull	1985–88	223	32	41	72	145

Current to 1998–99

5.8 A. Edmonton's Jari Kurri

Finnish sharpshooter Jari Kurri became the NHL's third 70-goal man in 1984–85 when he lit the lamp 71 times with the Edmonton Oilers. Kurri continued to sizzle in the playoffs, notching a record four hat tricks against Chicago in the semi-finals and equaling Reggie Leach's all-time mark of 19 goals in one playoff year.

5.9 A. Mike Bossy

Throughout Mike Bossy's wondrous career, he was forever in the shadow of Wayne Gretzky. While Bossy whacked home his 200th in his fourth season, after just 255 games, Gretzky needed only 242 contests to score goal No. 200. Mario Lemieux took 277 games, Brett Hull 280, and Eric Lindros 307, the fifth fewest games required by any 200-goal man in league history.

5.10 D. Mike Bossy

Wayne Gretzky's scoring totals made every other scorer of his era a hockey footnote, no matter what the achievement. Mike Bossy had an unprecedented nine 50-goal seasons. It was equaled by No. 99. But the New York Islanders center does have the edge in one category: his nine 50-goal years were consecutive; Gretzky's best was eight in a row.

5.11 B. Claude Lemieux

No matter how much criticism Claude Lemieux attracts for his subpar offensive numbers during the regular season, all is forgotten come playoff time. In postseason he is a model of consistency. Lemieux's 19 postseason game winners is second only to Gretzky's 24, and ahead of more obvious choices for playoff scoring champs, such as Maurice Richard (18 game winners), Mike Bossy (17) and Glenn Anderson (17).

Most Game-Winning Goals in Playoffs (Career)*		
Player	**Team**	**Goals**
Wayne Gretzky	Edm, LA, St. L, NYR	24
Claude Lemieux	Mtl, NJ, Col	19
Maurice Richard	Mtl	18
Mike Bossy	NYI	17
Glenn Anderson	Edm, Tor, NYR, St. L	17
Jean Beliveau	Mtl	15
Yvan Cournoyer	Mtl	15
Current to 1998–99		

5.12 A. The 1940s

Although Wayne Gretzky accomplished it an incredible three times, the first and only other seven-assist game in NHL history came courtesy of Billy "The Kid" Taylor. On March 16, 1947, Taylor caught fire, notching seven helpers in Detroit's 10–6 win over Chicago. Thanks to his playmaking skills, Taylor led the league in assists with 46 and finished third in the scoring race. His most-assists-in-a-game record lasted for a remarkable 33 years until equaled by the Great One, first on February 15, 1980, and twice later in the 1985–86 season.

5.13 C. Mario Lemieux

Wayne Gretzky achieved the NHL's longest and hottest scoring streak by blasting 153 points in 51 consecutive games between October 1983 and January 1984. Mario Lemieux holds the next longest streak, scoring in 46 straight games in 1989–90. Playing with terrible back pain and "at less than 50 per cent," according to Lemieux, he couldn't even tie his own skates for the last 20 games of the streak. Finally, on February 14, Mario was forced to the sidelines after racking up 39 goals and 64 assists for 103 points. He played only 59 games that season but finished with 123 points, fourth best in the league. The next best streak after Gretzky's and Lemieux's belongs to the Great One again, who totaled 108 points in a 39-game effort in 1985–86. Mats Sundin, Guy Lafleur and Steve Yzerman all have streaks of 30 games or less.

5.14 A. Bobby Orr

Few players mature so quickly that they become MVP candidates early in their NHL careers. In fact, the average age of most Hart Trophy recipients is 28. Wayne Gretzky was an exception, winning his first Hart in 1980 at age 19. The next youngest MVP winner is Bobby Orr, who was 21.9 years old when he snagged his first of three straight awards beginning in 1970. The Hart winner of 1995, Eric Lindros, was 22.4 years, Mario Lemieux was 22.8 years in 1988 and Bryan Trottier was 22.11 years in his Hart-winning season of 1979.

5.15 B. Two players

Besides Wayne Gretzky, only Jari Kurri and Mark Messier have reached the 100-playoff-goal plateau in the NHL. Gretzky's milestone marker came against Vancouver on May 7, 1993. Kurri also recorded his 100th during the 1993 playoffs, and Messier did it in 1995.

5.16 A. Gordie Howe and Jean Beliveau
Wayne Gretzky made 31 Stanley Cup finals appearances and scored a record 35 assists, topping Gordie Howe and Jean Beliveau, who each notched 32 helpers. Howe took 55 games and Beliveau 64 games to establish the original record of assists in finals action.

5.17 C. Steve Yzerman
The third-youngest sniper to score 1,000 points after Wayne Gretzky (age 23) and Mario Lemieux (age 26) is Steve Yzerman, who notched No. 1,000 during his 737th game on February 24, 1993. He was 27 years and nine months old, and in his 10th NHL season.

Player	Team	Date of 1000th	Game No.	Age
Wayne Gretzky	Edm	12/19/84	424	23.11
Mario Lemieux	Pit	03/24/92	513	26.5
Steve Yzerman	Det	02/24/93	737	27.9
Dale Hawerchuk	Buf	03/08/91	781	27.11
Mike Bossy	NYI	01/24/86	656	29.0
Denis Savard	Chi	03/11/90	727	29.2

The NHL's Youngest 1,000-Point Scorers*

Current to 1998–99

5.18 C. His 605th game
Mario Lemieux scored his 500th career goal in his 605th game, quicker than anyone else in NHL history except Wayne Gretzky (who did it in 575 games). The goal that came on October 26, 1995, in a 7–5 win over the New York Islanders, capped a three-goal performance. It was Lemieux's 32nd career hat trick.

5.19 D. Lanny McDonald in Toronto and Calgary
As of 1999, only two players have ever scored 200 goals with two NHL teams. While Phil Esposito, Norm Ullman and Frank Mahovlich just missed with their respective clubs, McDonald netted 219 goals as a Maple Leaf (1973 to 1979) and 215 goals with Calgary (1981 to 1989). Wayne Gretzky is the only other 200–200 scorer in NHL history, a feat he realized in 1993–94 after amassing 583 and 231 goals with Edmonton and Los Angeles respectively.

5.20 A. Gretzky scored three more goals
Mario Lemieux finished his 745-game career with 613 goals, just three fewer than Wayne Gretzky, who scored 616 times during his 745 games. Gretzky had a substantial lead with 1,774 points, compared to Lemieux's 1,494.

5.21 B. Between 400 and 500 games
Wayne Gretzky broke Guy Lafleur's old mark of 1,000 points in 720 games in his sixth season on December 19, 1984, with a six-point effort against the Los Angeles Kings. It was Wayne's 424th NHL game, a league record that almost certainly will never be broken.

5.22 B. Three points less (44 points)
If Wayne Gretzky set the standard by which Mario Lemieux is measured, then perhaps Lemieux's greatest scoring act is his 44-point playoff year in 1991, just three points behind Gretzky's all-time record of 47. During the 23 games, Lemieux fired a playoff-high 93 shots, scored 16 times and assisted on 28 others. In the 1991 finals against Minnesota, his most important goal came in Game 2. With Pittsburgh leading 2–1, he wheeled through center ice, split Minnesota defensemen Shawn Chambers and Neil Wilkinson with a deft move, then deked goalie Jon Casey and flipped a backhander between the posts as he fell to the ice. From that moment on, the Stars knew a healthy Lemieux was almost impossible to contain. For many, it was the play that turned the series.

5.23 C. Between 350 and 400 points

Wayne Gretzky not only owns many of the NHL's regular-season scoring records but many playoff marks as well, including most goals (122), most assists (260) and most points (382) in the postseason. The Great One's dominance is unlikely to be challenged anytime soon. His next closest rival, Mark Messier, has 295 points, a steep 87 playoff points behind Gretzky. Besides Messier, three other colleagues from Gretzky's Oilers days round out the top five: Jari Kurri (233 points), Glenn Anderson (214) and Paul Coffey (195). Gretzky racked up more playoff points than Jean Beliveau and Gordie Howe combined.

5.24 C. Five players

The true 50-goal-in-50-game player scores 50 times in his team's first 50 games of the season, rather than in *his* first 50 games of the season. An even stiffer test is the 50-in-fewer-than-50 category. Only five NHLers qualify in this class. Remarkably Wayne Gretzky did it three times before anyone else managed the feat. Mario Lemieux did it twice, and Brett Hull, Alexander Mogilny and Cam Neely once each. (Only Gretzky, Lemieux and Hull did their 50-in-fewer-than-50 feats in fewer than 50 team games.)

The NHL's 50-In-Fewer-Than-50 Goal Scorers*

Player	Team	Season	Date of 50th Goal	Player Game No.	Team Game No.
Wayne Gretzky	Edm	1981–82	30/12/8	39	39
Wayne Gretzky	Edm	1983–84	07/01/84	42	42
Wayne Gretzky	Edm	1984–85	26/01/85	49	49
Mario Lemieux	Edm	1988–89	20/01/89	44	46
Brett Hull	St. L	1990–91	25/01/91	49	49
Mario Lemieux	Pit	1992–93	21/03/93	48	72
Alex Mogilny	Buf	1992–93	03/02/93	46	53
Cam Neely	Bos	1993–94	07/03/94	44	66

Current to 1998–99

5.25 D. Two players

Both Bobby Hull and Phil Esposito came within a couple of games of the magical 50-in-50 mark, but it took Mike Bossy to do it again in 1980–81—36 years after Maurice Richard's 1944–45 feat and just one year before Wayne Gretzky set the all-time record of 50 in 39 during his dazzling 1981–82 season.

5.26 C. Adam Oates

Long past his glory days in Edmonton, Wayne Gretzky still dominated point totals between 1989–90 and 1998–99. In 713 games, Gretzky scored 1,020 points for a point-per-game average of 1.43. Second only to No. 99 during the 1990s is playmaker Adam Oates, who scored almost three times as many assists as goals while centering three of the league's top gunners: Brett Hull in St. Louis, Cam Neely in Boston and Peter Bondra in Washington.

The NHL's Top Scorers of the 1990s						
Player	Teams	GP	G	A	Pts.	PPG
Wayne Gretzky	LA, St. L, NYR	713	257	763	1,020	1.43
Adam Oates	St. L, Bos, Wsh	721	234	693	926	1.28
Steve Yzerman	Det	743	363	555	918	1.24
Joe Sakic	Que/Col	722	352	565	917	1.27
Brett Hull	St. L, Dallas	713	512	384	896	1.26
Pierre Turgeon	Buf, NYI, Mtl, St. L	721	349	518	867	1.20
Jaromir Jagr*	Pit	662	345	517	862	1.30

Jagr played one season less, since his career began in 1990–91. He is seventh in point totals but second to Gretzky in PPG during the decade.

GAME 5

CLOSE BUT NO CIGAR

Wayne Gretzky won a slew of silverware in his career. Every time he took home an Art Ross Trophy as the league's leading scorer or the Hart Trophy as regular-season MVP, someone else was denied that privilege. There are 15 NHLers who can say they were beaten out of hockey's most prestigious awards by the Great One. Once you've figured out who, find them in the puzzle reading down, across or diagonally. As with our example of Mike B-O-S-S-Y, connect the name using letters no more than once. Start with the letters printed in heavy type.

(Solutions are on page 121)

	C	E	**M**	L	L	Y	T	**S**	
S	S	O	U	**H**	E	A	E	U	**P**
I	**L**	I	F	F	S	**K**	T	Q	E
E	A	**L**	R	T	U	E	U	E	R
N	R	E	N	R	S	R	H	K	U
W	G	Y	M	I	T	R	C	W	O
A	X	U	E	O	N	T	E	A	**B**
T	Y	**T**	R	N	Y	O	I	**H**	V
U	I	**L**	E	S	R	E	I	R	O
	B–O–S			**F**	E	D	O	**D**	

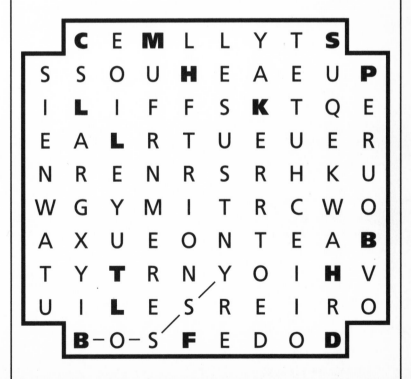

6

WITHOUT PEER
(WITH A FEW EXCEPTIONS)

During his exceptional hockey career, Wayne Gretzky didn't score in every game, win every scoring race or attain every award available to him every year. But his astronomical numbers in all scoring categories did deny a number of snipers the opportunity of establishing their own NHL records. Few were affected more than Mike Bossy. However, Bossy established a few records that outdistanced even No. 99. Gretzky scored 34 man-advantage goals in his career, one shy of the NHL mark held by Bossy, who popped in 35. In this chapter, Gretzky (or his team) is only one of four possible correct answers. The Great One didn't win everything; it just seems that way.

(Answers are on page 88)

6.1 Which sniper led the NHL in goal scoring the most times?
A. Gordie Howe
B. Bobby Hull
C. Phil Esposito
D. Wayne Gretzky

6.2 Who was the first player to win the Hart Trophy as the NHL's most valuable player by a unanimous vote?
A. Maurice Richard
B. Gordie Howe
C. Bobby Orr
D. Wayne Gretzky

6.3 Who is the youngest NHLer to score 100 points?
A. Jimmy Carson
B. Dale Hawerchuk
C. Mario Lemieux
D. Wayne Gretzky

6.4 Who set (and still holds) the Ontario Hockey Association (now the Ontario Hockey League) scoring record with 192 points in 1977–78?
A. Ottawa 67s' Bobby Smith
B. Oshawa Generals' Tony Tanti
C. Cornwall Royals' Doug Gilmour
D. Sault Ste. Marie Greyhounds' Wayne Gretzky

6.5 Wayne Gretzky took the fewest games to score 50 goals in a season. Which player was the fastest to reach 100 points from the start of a season?
A. Mario Lemieux
B. Pat LaFontaine
C. Steve Yzerman
D. Wayne Gretzky

6.6 Which team holds the NHL record for the longest undefeated streak from the start of the season?
A. The Montreal Canadiens in 1943–44
B. The Montreal Canadiens in 1972–73
C. The Edmonton Oilers in 1984–85
D. The Pittsburgh Penguins in 1994–95

6.7 Which player scored the most goals for an expansion team in its first NHL season?
A. Hartford's Blaine Stoughton in 1979–80
B. Florida's Bob Kudelski in 1993–94
C. Tampa Bay's Brian Bradley in 1992–93
D. Edmonton's Wayne Gretzky in 1979–80

6.8 In Wayne Gretzky's first NHL season, 1979–80, who won the Calder Trophy as NHL rookie of the year?
A. Ray Bourque
B. Mike Foligno
C. Peter Stastny
D. Wayne Gretzky

6.9 Who assisted on Mario Lemieux's famous series-winning goal at the 1987 Canada Cup?
A. Lemieux's goal went unassisted
B. Paul Coffey
C. Mark Messier
D. Wayne Gretzky

6.10 Who was the first NHLer to collect 100 assists in a season?
A. Bobby Orr
B. Stan Mikita
C. Marcel Dionne
D. Wayne Gretzky

6.11 What superstar didn't score a goal in his first NHL game?
A. Gordie Howe
B. Eric Lindros
C. Mario Lemieux
D. Wayne Gretzky

6.12 Before Wayne Gretzky scored 50 goals in fewer than 50 games, a WHA star did it. Who?
A. Marc Tardif of the WHA Quebec Nordiques
B. Robbie Ftorek of the WHA Phoenix Roadrunners
C. Anders Hedberg of the WHA Winnipeg Jets
D. Wayne Gretzky of the WHA Edmonton Oilers

6.13 Which NHL team scored the highest number of goals in one season?
A. The Boston Bruins in 1971–72
B. The Montreal Canadiens in 1976–77
C. The Edmonton Oilers in 1983–84
D. The Pittsburgh Penguins in 1990–91

6.14 Who is the NHL's all-time most consistent 30-plus goal scorer?
A. Mike Gartner
B. Bobby Hull
C. Phil Esposito
D. Wayne Gretzky

6.15 Who was the first hockey player to have his image appear on a Campbell's Soup can?
A. Gordie Howe
B. Maurice Richard
C. Bobby Orr
D. Wayne Gretzky

6.16 Who was the leading goal scorer in 1985–86, the year Wayne Gretzky set the all-time NHL record for most points in one season at 215 points?
A. Mario Lemieux
B. Jari Kurri
C. Mike Bossy
D. Wayne Gretzky

6.17 Who was the first player from an expansion team to lead the NHL in scoring?
A. Marcel Dionne
B. Bryan Trottier
C. Bobby Clarke
D. Wayne Gretzky

6.18 Who holds the all-time record for most goals in one season by a rookie in Canada's three junior leagues?
A. Pat LaFontaine
B. Tony Tanti
C. Don Murdoch
D. Wayne Gretzky

6.19 Who broke Maurice Richard's playoff career goal-scoring record first?
A. Jari Kurri
B. Glenn Anderson
C. Mike Bossy
D. Wayne Gretzky

6.20 Only a select few NHLers have ever had a season in which they either scored or assisted on half of their team's total goals. Who posted the highest single-season percentage of his club's total offense?
A. Steve Yzerman
B. Mario Lemieux
C. Marcel Dionne
D. Wayne Gretzky

6.21 Which NHLer registered the highest goal count in a Stanley Cup finals series?
A. Jean Beliveau
B. Mike Bossy
C. Wayne Gretzky
D. None of the above

6.22 What player's streak was broken because of the NHL lockout in 1994–95?
A. Mike Gartner's 15 consecutive 30-goal seasons
B. Patrick Roy's nine consecutive 20-win seasons
C. Wayne Gretzky's 14 consecutive All-Star appearances
D. All of the above

6.23 Who scored the greatest number of goals in one playoff series?
A. Jari Kurri
B. Tim Kerr
C. Reggie Leach
D. Wayne Gretzky

6.24 Since 1987, when each of the four playoff series required best-of-seven formats, what championship team won the Stanley Cup in the fewest number of postseason games? And how many games were played, if the minimum is 16 matches and the maximum is 28?
A. The Edmonton Oilers in 1988
B. The Pittsburgh Penguins in 1991
C. The Montreal Canadiens in 1993
D. The New Jersey Devils in 1995

6.25 Which dynasty team scored the most goals to win four Stanley Cups?
A. The Montreal Canadiens between 1964–65 and 1968–69
B. The Montreal Canadiens between 1975–76 and 1978–79
C. The New York Islanders between 1979–80 and 1982–83
D. The Edmonton Oilers between 1983–84 and 1987–88

6.26 Since Canada Cup competition began, which player has racked up the highest point totals in this international series?
A. Vladimir Krutov
B. Mark Messier
C. Sergei Makarov
D. Wayne Gretzky

6.27 As of 1999, who holds the NHL record for most playoff goals?
A. Jari Kurri
B. Maurice Richard
C. Mark Messier
D. Wayne Gretzky

6.28 Which player leads the NHL in All-Star Game points?
A. Mark Messier
B. Mario Lemieux
C. Gordie Howe
D. Wayne Gretzky

6.29 Who holds the NHL mark for the most points in a single playoff series?
A. Jean Beliveau
B. Rick Middleton
C. Brian Leetch
D. Wayne Gretzky

6.30 Who played in the most career NHL games?
A. Gordie Howe
B. Alex Delvecchio
C. Johnny Bucyk
D. Wayne Gretzky

6.31 Who holds the record for most career points in the Stanley Cup finals?
A. Jean Beliveau
B. Gordie Howe
C. Henri Richard
D. Wayne Gretzky

6.32 Who was the first Edmonton Oiler to win the Conn Smythe Trophy as MVP of the playoffs?
A. Grant Fuhr
B. Paul Coffey
C. Mark Messier
D. Wayne Gretzky

6.33 Who owns the NHL record for scoring points in the most consecutive playoff games?
A. Guy Lafleur
B. Bryan Trottier
C. Stan Mikita
D. Wayne Gretzky

6.34 As of 1999, which career goal-scoring leader has held his title the longest?
A. Howie Morenz
B. Gordie Howe
C. Maurice Richard
D. Wayne Gretzky

WITHOUT PEER
(WITH A FEW EXCEPTIONS)

Answers

6.1 **B. Bobby Hull**
One of the NHL's most famous No. 9s, Bobby Hull was not only among the league's speediest skaters, he also possessed the hardest shot in the game. Unlike Wayne Gretzky, who was

relatively small and slight, Hull had a remarkable physique. His powerful legs and muscular torso were built to play hockey. Hull's slap shot, unlike Gretzky's, was unrivaled. It was once clocked at a terrifying 118.3 miles per hour. Combining his high-velocity slapper with first-rate stickhandling and checking skills, the Golden Jet was unstoppable, winning scoring crowns, MVP awards and the Lady Byng Trophy as most gentlemanly player—all accolades that No. 99 attained. But Hull was a pure scorer and Gretzky, first and foremost, a playmaker who could also score. In the days before the Great One, few players matched Hull's superstar status. He leads all NHLers with seven goal-scoring titles.

The NHL's Top Goal-Scoring Champs

Player	Teams	Titles
Bobby Hull	Chicago	7
Phil Esposito	Boston	6
Wayne Gretzky	Edmonton	5
Maurice Richard	Montreal	5
Charlie Conacher	Toronto	5
Gordie Howe	Detroit	5

6.2 D. Wayne Gretzky
In 1981–82, Wayne Gretzky was unstoppable. He set new NHL records for goals (92), assists (120) and points (212), and finished 65 points ahead of runner-up Mike Bossy in the scoring race. In recognition of his exploits, the 63 voting members of the Professional Hockey Writers Association made the Great One a unanimous choice for the Hart Trophy, an NHL first.

6.3 B. Dale Hawerchuk
Dale Hawerchuk fulfilled all of the Winnipeg Jets' expectations as 1981's first overall draft pick, winning the Calder Trophy as top rookie and breaking the 100-point barrier at 18 years and 11 months old. Hawerchuk, who became the NHL's youngest 100-point man on March 24, 1982, beat Wayne Gretzky (19.2 years) in age by just three months. The only

other two teenagers to hit the century mark are Mario Lemieux (19.6 years) and Jimmy Carson (19.8 years).

6.4   A. Ottawa 67s' Bobby Smith
In 1977–78, 20-year-old Bobby Smith of the Ottawa 67s waged a yearlong battle with 17-year-old rookie Wayne Gretzky of the Sault Ste. Marie Greyhounds for the Ontario Hockey Association scoring title. When the smoke finally cleared, Smith, a three-year OHA veteran, had bested Gretzky by 10 points, 192 to 182. Both are still league records. Smith would enjoy a distinguished 16-year NHL career with Minnesota and Montreal, but he never outpointed the Great One again.

6.5   D. Wayne Gretzky
The ultimate team player, Wayne Gretzky routinely scored 100-point seasons. In 1983–84, he recorded the NHL's fastest 100 points in just 34 games. The following season he did it in 35 games. Mario Lemieux is the next fastest; he notched his quickest century mark in 36 games in 1988–89. Between them, Gretzky and Lemieux have combined to record the 12 fastest 100-point years.

6.6   C. The Edmonton Oilers in 1984–85
Led by Wayne Gretzky and Jari Kurri, the 1984–85 Edmonton Oilers produced the best season start by a team in NHL history, winning 12 games and tying three for a record undefeated streak of 15 games between October 11 and November 9, 1984. The next best streaking teams from the start of a season are the 1943–44 Montreal Canadiens (11 wins, three ties), the 1994–95 Pittsburgh Penguins (12 wins, one tie) and the 1972–73 Montreal Canadiens (nine wins, four ties).

6.7   A. Hartford's Blaine Stoughton in 1979–80
Blaine Stoughton scored 56 goals in the Hartford Whalers' inaugural NHL season—the most by a player on a first-year NHL expansion team. His 50th goal came on March 28, 1980, outpacing Wayne Gretzky, who scored his first No. 50 just five days later. That year Stoughton tied Buffalo's Danny Gare and

Los Angeles's Charlie Simmer for the 1979–80 goal-scoring lead—another first by an NHLer on a new team. Gretzky totaled 51 goals in 1979–80, Brian Bradley potted 42 in 1992–93 and Bob Kudelski hit the 40-goal mark in 1993–94.

6.8   A. Ray Bourque

Wayne Gretzky won almost every NHL award available to a forward, but like many of hockey's greatest (including Maurice Richard, Gordie Howe and Guy Lafleur), he was denied the Calder Trophy—for a reason other than quality of play. Because Gretzky played his first pro year (1978–79) in the WHA, the NHL disqualified him from the Calder rookie race in 1979–80. That opened the door to Boston's Ray Bourque, who began his Hall of Fame career with a 17–48–65 record and top rookie honors. The rookie issue wasn't soon forgotten. Gretzky has long argued that if the NHL considers his WHA experience a pro year, shouldn't his WHA points count in his career totals?

6.9   D. Wayne Gretzky

Many feel that the 1987 Canada Cup was the most dramatic tournament of all. All three games of the championship final between Canada and the Soviet Union finished in a 6–5 score. The Soviets won Game 1 on a goal by Alexander Smeak after five minutes of overtime. In Game 2, the clubs played 30 minutes of extra time before Mario Lemieux redirected a Wayne Gretzky shot past Soviet goalie Evgeny Belosheikin for the winning goal. In Game 3, Team Canada fell behind 3–0 and 4–2, but then rallied to take a 5–4 lead. They lost the lead again after the Soviets tied it. But with less than two minutes left in the game, Gretzky broke down the left wing, faked out a Soviet defender and slid the puck over to Lemieux, who buried it in the top corner to give Canada a 6–5 win and the tournament championship. The goal for Lemieux, just 22 years old, was a career turning point. "He [Gretzky] really showed me how to be a winner, how hard you have to work to become the No. 1 player in the world," Lemieux said. Gretzky recorded three goals and 18 assists in nine games, making him the tournament's leading scorer.

6.10 A. Bobby Orr

Boston's fabled No. 4 bagged 102 assists in 1970–71 to become the first NHLer to reach the century mark. In doing so, Bobby Orr broke his own record for assists (87), set the previous year. The bowlegged kid from Parry Sound completely revolutionized the role of the defenseman with his stick play and end-to-end dashes. Before Orr came along, Pat Stapleton held the NHL record for assists by a defenseman with 50. The only other players to break 100 assists in a season are Wayne Gretzky (11 times) and Mario Lemieux (once). Orr's 102-assist mark was snapped by Gretzky in 1980–81 when the Great One notched 109 helpers.

6.11 D. Wayne Gretzky

Wayne Gretzky didn't score his first NHL goal until his third game (October 14, 1979), a backhanded fan shot that dribbled through the legs of Vancouver's Glen Hanlon. Gordie Howe, wearing No. 17, scored (on Turk Broda) in his first NHL game on October 16, 1946. Mario Lemieux (first game, first shift, first shot on Pete Peeters) did the same deed on October 11, 1984, and Eric Lindros (Tom Barrasso) followed suit on October 6, 1992.

6.12 C. Anders Hedberg of the WHA Winnipeg Jets

The first player in professional hockey to break one of the game's most prestigious milestones, 50 goals in 50 games, was Anders Hedberg, who smashed Maurice Richard's mark set in 1945 by scoring 51 goals in 49 Winnipeg Jets games (his 47th match) in 1976–77. Playing with a cracked rib that had already sidelined him for two games and which was supposed to put him out indefinitely, the Jets' Swedish winger popped eight goals in Games 47 and 48, and then on February 6, 1977, against the Calgary Cowboys (Game 49), he scored goals 49th, 50th and 51st goals, finally surpassing the Rocket's 32-year record. In Wayne Gretzky's first and only WHA season, he scored 46 goals and was the league's top rookie of the year.

6.13 C. The Edmonton Oilers in 1983–84

Using coach Glen Sather's fire-wagon style of offense, the 1983–84 Edmonton Oilers pumped an NHL-record 446 goals past opposing netminders during an 80-game schedule. Wayne Gretzky led the offensive barrage, ringing up 87 goals, followed by Glenn Anderson's 54 red lights and Jari Kurri's 52. Defenseman Paul Coffey scored 40 times and Mark Messier 37 times. The watershed year produced another record high. So prolific were the Oilers in 1983–84 that even netminder Grant Fuhr had a great offensive year, compiling an NHL goalie record of 14 assists.

6.14 A. Mike Gartner

Bobby Hull, Phil Esposito and Wayne Gretzky each recorded 13 straight 30-plus-goal seasons, but Mike Gartner went two better, earning his 15th consecutive 30-plus-goal year in 1993–94. Gartner scored at least 33 goals in each of those 15 seasons and hit the 40-goal plateau nine times. He retired with a record 17 30-plus-goal seasons, three more than any other NHLer.

6.15 D. Wayne Gretzky

The term *superstar* took on a new meaning for Wayne Gretzky in 1996–97 when he became the first person to appear on a Campbell's Soup label. The image of Gretzky—clad in a generic uniform—along with his signature, appeared on 50 million labels of Campbell's Chunky.

6.16 B. Jari Kurri

Despite a record-setting 215-point season in 1985–86, Wayne Gretzky didn't lead the league in goals. His 52 goals ranked third behind Mike Bossy's 61-goal performance and teammate Jari Kurri's 68-goal league high. Gretzky scored 163 assists (another all-time NHL record), many of them helping Kurri net his 68-goal count.

6.17 B. Bryan Trottier

The New York Islanders lucked out by selecting Bryan Trottier 22nd overall in the 1974 Amateur Draft. He proved to be the best player in the entire draft. A key member of the Islanders' four championship teams in the early 1980s, Trottier became the first player from a postexpansion team to top the NHL in scoring when he collected 134 points in 1978–79.

6.18 A. Pat LaFontaine

American-born Pat LaFontaine cut a wide swath through the Quebec Major Junior Hockey League in 1982–83, his rookie year. The St. Louis, Missouri, native scored 104 goals in 70 games with the Verdun Junior Canadiens. LaFontaine learned hockey in Detroit before playing junior in Montreal, amassing more goals that any other freshman in Canadian junior-hockey history. Next best are: Don Murdoch with 82 goals for Medicine Hat (Western Hockey League) in 1974–75; Tony Tanti with 81 goals for Oshawa (Ontario Hockey League) in 1980–81; and Wayne Gretzky with 70 goals for Sault Ste. Marie (Ontario Hockey Association) in 1977–78.

6.19 C. Mike Bossy

It took 26 years of postseason play before anyone beat Maurice Richard's career record for most goals during the playoffs. The Rocket's 82-goal mark, set in 1960, was finally eclipsed during the 1986 playoffs by Mike Bossy, who scored his 83rd career goal against the Washington Capitals' Pete Peeters on April 12, 1986. Bossy's career mark of 85 playoff goals was surpassed three years later by Wayne Gretzky during the 1989 postseason.

6.20 B. Mario Lemieux

Only four NHLers have ever had a season in which they figured in half their team's total goals. Joe Malone and Cy Denneny did it in the NHL's early days when players often remained on the ice the entire game. Among modern-day players, only Mario Lemieux and Wayne Gretzky have duplicated the feat. Lemieux's 1988–89 performance is in a class by itself. He either scored or assisted on an amazing 57.3 per cent of the goals scored by the Pittsburgh Penguins that season—the highest percentage in NHL history. Despite his astonishing numbers, Lemieux didn't win the league MVP award in 1988–89. It went to Gretzky, who scored the same number of assists as Lemieux, but 31 fewer goals. Gretzky's MVP triumph over the high-scoring Lemieux was due to the fact that No. 99, in his first year with Los Angeles, took the Kings from being the fourth-worst team in the NHL to the fourth-best club—a 23-point jump in one season.

The NHL's League-Leading Scorers by Percentage-Against-Team Scoring*

Player	Year	G	A	Pts	Team Goals	Pct
Mario Lemieux	1988–89	85	114	199	347	57.3
Joe Malone	1919–20	39	9	48	91	52.7
Mario Lemieux	1987–88	70	98	168	319	52.7
Wayne Gretzky	1984–85	73	135	208	401	51.9
Wayne Gretzky	1981–82	92	120	212	417	50.8
Cy Denneny	1924–25	27	15	42	83	50.6
Wayne Gretzky	1985–86	52	163	215	426	50.5
Wayne Gretzky	1980–81	55	109	164	328	50.0

*Current to 1998–99

6.21 D. None of the above

Three players—Jean Beliveau, Mike Bossy and Wayne Gretzky —all registered seven goals in one Stanley Cup finals. But two other players from old-time hockey scored more in final round history. Toronto's Alf Skinner potted eight goals in five games in 1918's Cup finals against the Vancouver Millionaires. Then, four years later, another Toronto forward, Babe Dye, tallied nine of his club's 16 goals, including two game winners, to establish a 78-year record that remains unbroken today.

6.22 D. All of the above

There were plenty of broken records due to the 1994–95 lockout-shortened 48-game schedule. Not only did Mike Gartner miss his first 30-goal season in 15 years (he scored just 12 in 1994–95), but Patrick Roy, who won 17 games that season, ended his nine-year reign of 20-win seasons. Wayne Gretzky's record 14 straight All-Star appearances was also halted. A number of other streaks were broken because of the labor dispute. For the first time in a quarter century of NHL hockey, there were no 100-point or 50-goal scorers, nor any 100-point teams.

6.23 A. Jari Kurri

No team has ever turned on red lights faster than the Wayne Gretzky-led Edmonton Oilers. And no Edmonton team has been more prodigious in any playoff series than the 1985 squad that averaged 7.3 goals per game against Chicago in the 1985 Western Conference finals. A multitude of records were set, including, first and foremost, Jari Kurri's 12-goal performance, the highest individual goal count in one postseason round. Kurri had two hat tricks and a four-goal game, another NHL mark. And Gretzky didn't come away empty-handed. As Kurri's setup man, he notched a league-record 14 assists. Team and league records were also set in the wild point-filled series. An NHL-record 69 goals were scored, with the Oilers outscoring the Hawks 44–25 in six games. Edmonton notched two double-digit games, an NHL first in modern history. Trying to stem the puck parade was Blackhawks goalie Murray Bannerman, who earned the distinction of allowing the most playoffs goals in one series in Chicago's 70-year history. The Blackhawks, with Denis Savard, Steve Larmer and Doug Wilson, combined to average more than four goals per game. The shootout fest produced another NHL record: the most goals by both teams in one playoff series—11.5 goals per game.

General manager Glen Sather's brand of wide-open hockey worked to prefection: let them score, because we'll score more.

6.24 A. The Edmonton Oilers in 1988
The Edmonton Oilers won the 1988 Stanley Cup in 18 games, losing just twice during their best-of-seven, four-round playoff series, once to Winnipeg in the division semifinals and another in the conference finals to the Detroit Red Wings. Edmonton won the other two series, the division finals against Calgary and the Cup finals versus Boston, both in four games straight.

6.25 C. The New York Islanders between 1979–80 and 1982–83
Because of the sheer volume of team and individual records established by Wayne Gretzky and the Edmonton Oilers during their dynasty years of the 1980s, we tend to overlook the scoring prowess of the New York Islanders in their glory years. Between 1980 and 1983, the Isles, led by Mike Bossy, Bryan Trottier and Denis Potvin, scored an unreal 87 goals in just 19 final-series games to capture four Stanley Cups. By comparison, Edmonton's powerhouse needed more games (22) and scored fewer goals (85) to win its four championships.

6.26 D. Wayne Gretzky
Gretzky, a 15-year-old junior sensation, watched from the stands when the world's best players competed in the first Canada

Cup in 1976. Five years later he was playing his Canadian heart out against the top-rated Czechs, Finns and Russians. With four Canada Cups (1981, 1984, 1987 and 1991) and one World Cup (1996) under his belt, the Great One truly ranks as the greatest in the world, thanks to his 20 goals and 63 points in 38 games. Gretzky never ranked any lower than second in scoring during those five series.

6.27 D. Wayne Gretzky

The NHL record for most playoff goals was, for a long time, a three-way battle among former Edmonton Oilers teammates Wayne Gretzky, Mark Messier and Jari Kurri. At the time of his retirement, No. 99 led all scorers with 122 playoff goals, followed by Messier's 109. The Great One reached double digits in goals scored six times and had his best season in 1984–85 when he totaled 17 goals in 18 games. Gretzky never failed to score in any playoff in which he participated. His scoring average after 208 playoff games is a whopping 59 per cent.

6.28 D. Wayne Gretzky

Wayne Gretzky solidified his lead in All-Star points at the 1999 NHL All-Star Game in Tampa Bay. He scored a goal and assisted on two others (by Mark Recchi and Rob Blake) to boost his All-Star numbers to 25 points (13 goals, 12 assists)— a safe distance from Mario Lemieux (20), Gordie Howe (19) and Mark Messier (17). Gretzky's All-Star point mark is one of the few records that has his goal count outnumbering his assist count.

6.29 B. Rick Middleton

An overtime goal by Brad Park lifted the Boston Bruins past the Buffalo Sabres in Game 7 of the 1983 Adams Division finals, but the real hero of the series was Rick Middleton. The shifty Bruin forward repeatedly bamboozled Buffalo's defense, collecting a single-series record 19 points on five goals and 14 assists. Wayne Gretzky missed this record by one point, scoring four goals and 14 assists for 18 points in 1985's conference finals blitz against Chicago.

6.30 A. Gordie Howe

One of the few records Wayne Gretzky hasn't added to his collection is in the most-games-played category. He would have had to play 280 games or almost four more seasons injury-free to equal Gordie Howe's record. Under those circumstances, Gretzky would have celebrated his retirement at age 42 in 2003. Wisely he left hockey in 1998–99 while he was still near the top of his game. He is fourth all-time in games played (1,487) behind Howe (1,767), Alex Delvecchio (1,549) and Johnny Bucyk (1,540).

6.31 A. Jean Beliveau

Unlike Wayne Gretzky, who failed to make the playoffs in his last two seasons, Jean Beliveau went out on top, captaining the Montreal Canadiens to the Stanley Cup in 1970–71, the 10th of his illustrious career. Beliveau finished the playoffs with six goals and a then-record 16 assists, leaving the sport as the all-time leader in playoff points. He has since been eclipsed in that category, but still holds the mark for most points in the finals. Beliveau has 62 points, compared to Gretzky's 53. But while the great Canadiens center played in 64 final appearances, No. 99 was in only 31 games.

6.32 C. Mark Messier

The Edmonton Oilers thwarted the New York Islanders' bid to win a fifth consecutive Stanley Cup in 1984, dethroning the NHL champions in five games in the finals. Wayne Gretzky led all playoff marksmen with 35 points, but the Conn Smythe Trophy as the playoff MVP went to Mark Messier, whose grit and tenacity sparked the young Oilers to their first Cup.

6.33 B. Bryan Trottier

The New York Islanders' championship squads of the 1980s boasted a host of talented performers, but none contributed more to the club's success than Bryan Trottier. The hard-driving center counted a point in 27 consecutive playoff games between 1980 and 1982, setting a record that no other player has approached. Even Wayne Gretzky's point-scoring streak of 19 straight games in 1988 and 1989 is a distant second. Trottier logged 42 points (16 goals, 26 assists) in those 27 games, but he was especially impressive during the 1981 playoffs when he scored a point in all 18 games the Islanders played, setting the longest consecutive point-scoring streak in one postseason. Gretzky follows Trottier in this category, but just by one game. Trottier scored 29 points in 18 straight games; Gretzky tallied 41 points in 17 games.

6.34 B. Gordie Howe

There have only been seven career goal-scoring champs in NHL history. In 1994 Wayne Gretzky, the seventh, took over from Gordie Howe, who had owned the NHL crown for 30 years since dethroning Maurice Richard in 1963–64. Howe's three-decade reign is the longest, but Gretzky could very well upset that mark. How likely is it that someone will top Gretzky's 894-goal count? That future gunner would have to do it before the year 2024 (for Howe to maintain the longest all-time scoring reign).

The NHL's Career Goal-Scoring Champs*

Player	Year Record Set	Total Goals	Length of Reign
Joe Malone	1917–18	44	1 year
Cy Denneny	1918–19	54	1 year
Joe Malone	1919–20	146	4 years
Cy Denneny	1922–23	246	12 years
Howie Morenz	1933–34	270	4 years
Nels Stewart	1936–37	324	16 years
Maurice Richard	1952–53	544	12 years
Gordie Howe	1963–64	801	30 years
Wayne Gretzky	1993–94	894	6 years +

Current to 1998–99

GAME 6
NO. 99'S LAST STANLEY CUP

In this game, 27 Edmonton Oilers players and managers from Wayne Gretzky's last Stanley Cup victory in 1988 appear in the puzzle horizontally, vertically or backward. Some are easily found, such as GRETZKY; others require a more careful search. After you've circled all 27 names, read the remaining 12 letters in descending order to reveal our hidden phrase. It describes an unusual occurrence that suspended Game 4 of the finals against Boston.

(Solutions are on page 121)

```
K M O O B E K U E B G I
U H Y E L R O S C M R N
R U M U C K L E R E E U
R D R P S M I T H B E M
I D A O P W E T M R N D
L Y N F O A A O M T M N
L K F I C S C E I A A A
A Z O L K A S K C N C L
N T R O L S K G N D T L
T E D W I A R N O E A E
R R L E N E H A S R V L
U G R E G G U N P S I C
O U N O T R F N M O S C
C E R N O T C A I N H M
I K S Y N L E H S U R K
```

7

THE FINAL 99 HOURS

Wayne Gretzky's exit from hockey couldn't have been better orchestrated had Hollywood produced it. He had all but announced the sensational news during his last four days of hockey. Under the glare of intense media speculation, the big question kept surfacing: Was the game's greatest player about to retire? The hockey world watched and waited in stunned disbelief. Luckily he had one game left in his homeland, Canada. Then it was back to Madison Square Garden in New York, the greatest city an athlete can play in. Gretzky might have slowed a bit on the ice, but he hadn't lost his timing. He was even retiring in the year of his number. His New York farewell literally raised the bar on sports retirements. Oh, he could have scored the game's winning goal or won the Stanley Cup a final time, but those two games were a wonder to watch. In his last news conference, Gretzky was asked 41 questions. Here are a few of our own.

(Answers are on page 108)

7.1 When Jaromir Jagr apologized to Wayne Gretzky by saying "I didn't mean to do that," during No. 99's last game in April 1999, what was the Pittsburgh Penguin referring to?
A. A goal
B. A body check
C. A fight
D. A comment on national television

7.2 How many more career NHL points does Wayne Gretzky have than runner-up Gordie Howe? (Howe has 1,850 points.)
A. Between 400 and 600 points
B. Between 600 and 800 points
C. Between 800 and 1,000 points
D. More than 1,000 points

7.3 Of Wayne Gretzky's record 50 hat tricks, how many did he score as an Edmonton Oiler?
A. 34 hat tricks
B. 37 hat tricks
C. 40 hat tricks
D. 43 hat tricks

7.4 How many regular-season games did Wayne Gretzky miss during his 20-year career?
A. Fewer than 100 games
B. Between 100 and 200 games
C. Between 200 and 300 games
D. More than 300 games

7.5 What was the last Canadian city Wayne Gretzky played in?
A. Ottawa
B. Vancouver
C. Toronto
D. Edmonton

7.6 Which broadcaster broke the story of Wayne Gretzky's retirement?
A. Ron MacLean
B. John Davidson
C. Mike Lange
D. Don Cherry

7.7 Against whom did Wayne Gretzky score his final NHL goal?
A. St. Louis's Grant Fuhr
B. The New York Islanders' Wade Flaherty
C. Dallas's Ed Belfour
D. Buffalo's Dominik Hasek

7.8 How many hockey sticks did Wayne Gretzky use in his final NHL game?
A. 10 sticks
B. 20 sticks
C. 30 sticks
D. 40 sticks

7.9 Who did Wayne Gretzky say is the best player he ever played with and played against in his career?
A. With Jari Kurri, and against Mike Bossy
B. With Bernie Nicholls, and against Steve Yzerman
C. With Glenn Anderson, and against Pavel Bure
D. With Mark Messier, and against Mario Lemieux

7.10 How many times was Wayne Gretzky named Player of the Week during his 20-year NHL career?
A. 24 times
B. 44 times
C. 64 times
D. 84 times

7.11 What brand of hockey stick did Wayne Gretzky become most closely associated with during the latter part of his career?
A. Koho
B. Sher-Wood
C. Easton
D. Titan

7.12 During his entire hockey career, how many points did Wayne Gretzky score in international competition?
A. Between 50 and 75 points
B. Between 75 and 100 points
C. Between 100 and 125 points
D. More than 125 points

7.13 How many times did Wayne Gretzky appear on the cover of *Sports Illustrated*?
A. Eight times
B. 12 times
C. 16 times
D. 20 times

7.14 In which road arena did Wayne Gretzky score the most goals?
A. Winnipeg Arena
B. Edmonton's Northlands Coliseum
C. Toronto's Maple Leaf Gardens
D. Detroit's Joe Louis Arena

7.15 How many NHLers played with and later coached Wayne Gretzky at the pro level?
A. Only one, Larry Robinson
B. Two NHLers
C. Three NHLers
D. Four NHLers

7.16 Among the 49 arenas in which Wayne Gretzky played, how many venues did he fail to record a point in?
A. None—Gretzky had a point in every rink in which he played
B. Only one arena
C. Three arenas
D. Five arenas

7.17 Against which NHL team did Wayne Gretzky score the highest percentage of goals?
A. The Toronto Maple Leafs
B. The Vancouver Canucks
C. The Detroit Red Wings
D. The Colorado Avalanche–Quebec Nordiques

7.18 What is the most number of points Wayne Gretzky has scored against one NHL team in his career?
A. 100 to 150 points
B. 150 to 200 points
C. 200 to 250 points
D. More than 250 points

7.19 According to Wayne Gretzky, what was his greatest goal?
A. His first NHL goal
B. His 50th goal in 39 games
C. An overtime playoff winner
D. His 802nd goal

7.20 How many fights was Wayne Gretzky penalized for?
A. None
B. Three fights
C. Six fights
D. 12 fights

7.21 In which month of the hockey season did Wayne Gretzky score his most goals?
A. October
B. December
C. March
D. April

7.22 What was Wayne Gretzky's career plus-minus rating?
A. Between +200 and +300
B. Between +300 and +400
C. Between +400 and +500
D. More than +500

7.23 How many NHL records did Wayne Gretzky lead or share the lead in upon his retirement?
A. Fewer than 40 NHL records
B. Between 40 and 50 NHL records
C. Between 50 and 60 NHL records
D. More than 60 NHL records

7.24 Wayne Gretzky's final career point came off a goal from which New York Rangers player in April 1999?
A. Adam Graves
B. John MacLean
C. Brian Leetch
D. Wayne Gretzky himself

7.25 According to Wayne Gretzky, what was the greatest game he ever played?
A. An NHL regular-season game
B. An NHL playoff game
C. An NHL All-Star Game
D. An international game

7.26 What gift did Wayne Gretzky receive after taking off his skates for the final time?
A. A car
B. Golf shoes
C. A leather couch
D. A rocking chair

7.27 What was Wayne Gretzky's most cherished hockey memory?
A. Scoring his first NHL goal
B. Amassing 50 goals in 39 games
C. Winning his first Stanley Cup
D. Scoring goal No. 802 to become the NHL's all-time scoring leader

THE FINAL 99 HOURS
Answers

7.1 A. A goal
Wayne Gretzky lost his last NHL game, in a 2–1 New York Rangers defeat, to the Pittsburgh Penguins when Jaromir Jagr scored the overtime winner. According to Gretzky, "Maybe it was only fitting that the best young player in the game scored the goal in overtime. Everyone talks about passing torches. Well, he caught it." And did the finest one-on-one player in the game apologize? "Yeah," Gretzky commented, "he said, 'I didn't mean to do that.' That's what I used to say, I told him."

7.2 D. More than 1,000 points
Wayne Gretzky scored 2,857 career NHL points, a dazzling 54 per cent more than second-place Gordie Howe's 1,850. Equally

impressive is the assist totals that No. 99 amassed over his nearest rival, Paul Coffey. Gretzky had 2,223 career assists, 78 per cent better than Coffey's 1,238 total. Those percentage differentials are by far the greatest in a major category in any pro sports record book.

7.3 D. 43 hat tricks
Wayne Gretzky leads all NHLers in regular-season hat tricks with 50, 43 of them coming as an Edmonton Oiler. He scored his 49th on November 23, 1991, then proceeded to go the next 396 contests without one. His 50th and last three-goal game finally came against the Vancouver Canucks on October 11, 1997, when he was a New York Ranger. Longtime division rivals of two Gretzky teams, Edmonton and Los Angeles, the Canucks bore a disproportionate number of milestones by the Great One, including his first NHL goal; his 200th, the fastest in NHL history; his 500th; his 611th, to surpass Bobby Hull; and his record-setting 802nd.

7.4 A. Fewer than 100 games
Over his 20-season NHL career, Wayne Gretzky missed only 97 games. The highest number, 39 matches, was in 1992–93. The Great One played eight complete seasons.

7.5 A. Ottawa
Wayne Gretzky's last NHL game on Canadian soil was in Ottawa, his homeland's capital. The city was abuzz and tickets were impossible to find. Federal cabinet ministers begged for seats, and Prime Minister Jean Chrétien tried to rejig his schedule to be at the game. Wayne's parents, Phyllis and Walter Gretzky, were flown in and a postgame press conference was scheduled. The New York Rangers tied the Ottawa Senators 2–2, but No. 99 didn't score. Nor did he confirm his retirement, saving the big splash for his final match in New York three days later. Senators goalie Ron Tugnutt said before the Ottawa game: "I'm hoping for a bench-clearing brawl during the warm-up, so I can go out and grab his stick.... His hands are still there. They haven't gone anywhere. It's strange

to say, but he's more dangerous behind the net than anyone else. It's a talent no one else has."

7.6   B. John Davidson

Just weeks before the conclusion of the 1998–99 season, John Davidson announced on the Madison Square Garden network and later on Fox's *Game of the Week* and then on CBC's *Hockey Night in Canada* that there was a better-than-80-per-cent chance that Wayne Gretzky would retire. What tipped Davidson off? Sticks and pucks. Davidson observed that No. 99 was stockpiling memorabilia. The all-time leading scorer in the game was using more sticks and saving more pucks than usual and storing them away. Davidson's deduction proved correct. Gretzky confirmed what Davidson had suspected: he was considering leaving the game. From there, a media frenzy of will-he-or-won't-he reports set the stage for the Great One's last two NHL contests in Ottawa and New York.

7.7   B. The New York Islanders' Wade Flaherty

On March 29, 1999, Wayne Gretzky scored his final NHL goal against Wade Flaherty. It came unassisted at 17:53 of the third period and broke a 1–1 deadlock in a game the New York Rangers eventually won 3–1. It was No. 99's final game winner of his marvelous career, and a rare memorable moment in a lackluster final season. The historic goal proved to be a milestone of greater significance. It was Gretzky's 1,072nd career WHA and NHL goal, giving him one more goal than Gordie Howe's all-time record of 1,071 goals. The Great One's last career goal made him the most prolific goal scorer in major professional hockey.

7.8   D. 40 sticks

In his final NHL contest on April 18, 1999, Wayne Gretzky used as many as 40 sticks, many of which he would keep to donate to charitable functions or pass on to friends and teammates. Gretzky wore three sweaters in the game (one he kept, another went to New York general manager Neil Smith and the third jersey to an undetermined lucky soul). In his last game, a 2–1 loss to Pittsburgh, Gretzky played 22 shifts or 22 minutes, 30 seconds. He had just two shots on net and recorded his final NHL point off the lone Ranger goal. He won 10 face-offs and lost four. His best pass was a backhanded seeing-eye pass to Niklas Sundstrom, who set up John MacLean. Tom Barrasso stopped the low shot. Gretzky's best scoring chance came on a two-on-one break, but MacLean waited too long and slipped the puck behind Gretzky and into the corner.

7.9   D. With Mark Messier, and against Mario Lemieux
In Wayne Gretzky's pregame speech during his final career game at Madison Square Garden, the Great One said to the crowd: "I feel so lucky that I was able to play in the National Hockey League. I feel so fortunate to have played with some of the game's greatest players ... and the best player I ever played with—Mark Messier. With the best player I ever played against—Mario Lemieux." Gretzky and Messier won four Stanley Cups together. Gretzky and Lemieux are the only two players in NHL history with 2.00 points-per-game averages in their careers.

7.10 B. 44 times
No player has captured more weekly honors since the inception of Player of the Week (in 1980–81) than Wayne Gretzky. His career total doubles the second-highest count, held by Mario Lemieux. Gretzky earned his first Player of the Week award on January 12, 1981, after recording 10 points (three goals, seven assists) in three games. In 1982–83, he won the weekly honor a record eight times and repeated the effort in 1983–84. His best weekly total was a 17-point week (seven goals, 10 assists) from December 13 to 19, 1983. To cap his career, the Great One was named Player of the Week during his last week of NHL play, April 12 to 18, 1999. It was Gretzky's 44th weekly honor.

7.11 C. Easton
Wayne Gretzky used at least five stick brands dating back to his minor-league days in Ontario. On April 10, 1974, he scored his milestone 1,000th minor-league goal with a Koho

Champion Hook; he was 13 years old and playing for Turk-stra Lumber. Four years later, in February 1978, Gretzky used a Sher-Wood P.M.P. 5001 to net his 138th point, the OHA record for most points by a rookie, with the Junior A Sault Ste. Marie Greyhounds. Gretzky switched to Titan and the Titan TPM2020 when he joined the WHA and NHL. He recorded all 1,851 points (to equal Gordie Howe's career mark) with a Titan stick. Compared to other snipers with their deeply curved blades and soft-flexing shafts, Gretzky chose a moderate curve and rigid shaft. But the rigidity made the stick heavy—a negative factor for a player who cut and trimmed every piece of equipment just to save precious ounces. In the early 1990s, Easton caught Gretzky's eye with its stiff, lightweight aluminum shaft and perfectly curved blade. When the camera lights hit the shaft, it shone like a *Star Wars* lightsaber. Gretzky's last stick was a Hespeler composite shaft. "No flex," reported the Great One in *The Hockey News*. "About a 4.5 lie. Cut just under my chin. Heel-to-tip tape job, baby powder. I used a gripper on the shaft end because I wanted the exact same knob every game."

7.12 C. Between 100 and 125 points
Wayne Gretzky played in nine international series between 1978's World Junior Championships and the Olympics Games in 1998. In 64 games, he scored 34 goals and 68 assists for 102 points.

Wayne Gretzky's International Statistics						
Event	GP	G	A	TP	PIM	Place
1979 World Juniors	6	8	9	17	2	4th
1981 Canada Cup	7	5	7	12	2	2nd
1982 Worlds	10	6	8	14	0	3rd
1984 Canada Cup	8	5	7	12	2	1st
1987 Rendez-Vous	2	0	4	4	0	
1987 Canada Cup	9	3	18	21	2	1st
1991 Canada Cup	7	4	8	12	2	1st
1996 World Cup	7	3	3	6	2	2nd
1998 Olympics	6	0	4	4	2	4th
Totals	62	34	68	102	14	

7.13 C. 16 times

No player on ice was covered more by *Sports Illustrated* than Wayne Gretzky. From his early days in Edmonton when *SI* billed him as the Great Gretzky to his farewell skate in New York, No. 99 appeared on *SI*'s coveted front cover an unprecedented 16 times, including 12 exclusive covers and four covers on which his photo wasn't the primary image. In 1982, his third cover, Gretzky was named *SI*'s Sportsman of the Year. Bobby Hull and Bobby Orr follow Gretzky with five *SI* covers each, while Gordie Howe notched four cover appearances. When the Great One retired, he was No. 8 on the list of all-time cover subjects, one behind Pete Rose and two ahead of Mike Tyson, Bill Walton and Arnold Palmer. By comparison, Gretzky's mug graced the cover of *The Hockey News* 70 times.

7.14 A. Winnipeg Arena
Gretzky scored goals in 42 of the 49 arenas in which he played. His greatest goal count came in Winnipeg at the Arena where he totaled 38 regular-season goals. Where *didn't* the Great One net a goal? He never scored at Ottawa's Corel Centre, Miami's National Car Rental Center, Nashville's Arena, Sacramento's ARCO Arena, Springfield's Civic Center (in Massachusetts), Chicago's United Center, and Montreal's Molson Centre.

7.15 B. Two NHLers
During his 21-year professional career in the WHA and the NHL, Wayne Gretzky played under 11 coaches, two of whom also teamed with the Great One at one time or another. Larry Robinson played with and coached Gretzky during the 1990s in Los Angeles; Colin Campbell, No. 99's last coach, was a defenseman with Edmonton in 1979–80. Gretzky's other bench bosses were Pat Stapleton (his first pro coach in the WHA in 1978–79), Glen Sather, Bryan Watson, John Muckler, Robbie Ftorek, Tom Webster, Barry Melrose, Rogatien Vachon and Mike Keenan.

7.16 B. Only one arena
Wayne Gretzky scored at least one point in 48 of the 49 NHL rinks in which he played. The only arena that failed to witness a No. 99 point was the Springfield Civic Center, home of his hockey hero Gordie Howe and the Hartford Whalers during Gretzky's first season.

7.17 A. The Toronto Maple Leafs
Wayne Gretzky's best goal-scoring percentage was against
Toronto. He scored a goal in 87.3 per cent of the home and
away games against the Maple Leafs. In those 63 contests,
Gretzky notched 55 goals, slightly better than the 87-per-cent
mark (69 games and 60 goals) against his onetime team, the
Los Angeles Kings. When No. 99 played in Maple Leaf Gardens, his favorite road arena, he totaled 30 career goals and
47 assists in 30 appearances there, the most by any visiting
player in the 68-year history of the famous rink.

7.18 C. 200 to 250 points
Every time Wayne Gretzky played the Vancouver Canucks, he
came away with more than two points per game. The Great
One scored 239 points in 117 games against the Canucks, the
highest point number he tallied against any NHL team.

7.19 C. An overtime playoff winner
According to Wayne Gretzky, his greatest goal among his 1,000-
plus markers in regular-season and playoff action is the one he
scored on April 21, 1988. It was one of No. 99's few overtime
winners in postseason, and it came shorthanded on a long slap
shot against Calgary's Mike Vernon in Game 2 of the Smythe
Division finals. The 5–4 win over the archrival Flames gave the
Edmonton Oilers the momentum to sweep both Calgary 4–0
in the series and Boston 4–0 in the Cup finals.

7.20 B. Three fights
Wayne Gretzky was sent to the penalty box on three occa-
sions for fighting—all during his Edmonton Oilers days and
all at home in that city. On March 14, 1980, he was penal-
ized for a scuffle with Doug Lecuyer of Chicago; on Decem-
ber 22, 1982, he took on Minnesota's Neal Broten; and on
March 7, 1984, he and Bob Murray tangled. Ironically the
Broten fight happened on the same night that No. 99 received
Sports Illustrated's prestigious 1982 Sportsman of the Year
Award in a pregame ceremony.

7.21 B. December

In the seven-month playing period between October and April, Wayne Gretzky scored more goals in October (126), November (154), December (157), March (144) and April (25) than any other NHLer in league history. Gordie Howe is ahead in the months of January (154, compared to the Great One's 152) and February (151–136), with No. 99 second in both.

7.22 D. More than +500

Wayne Gretzky recorded 14 seasons in the plus column and six in the minus. He led the league in plus-minus numbers four times, including in his best year, 1984–85, with a sizzling +98. The Great One's worst plus-minus count came in 1993–94 when he won his last Art Ross Trophy with 130 points. Gretzky accumulated a -25 with Los Angeles that year. At the time of his retirement, No. 99 topped all active NHLers with a +518 rating. Ray Bourque was second with +453.

7.23 D. More than 60 NHL records

No player has ever been such a force in any professional league the way Wayne Gretzky has. He rewrote the record books and the history of the NHL. Between regular-season and playoff action, No. 99 holds 61 league marks in most categories of career, season, game and single-period records. He leads the NHL in all individual scoring records (goals, assists and points) and certain per-game scoring averages, scoring plateaus, three-or-more goal games and scoring streaks.

7.24 C. Brian Leetch

On April 18, 1999, in his final NHL game, Wayne Gretzky pegged his 2,857th and final career point on a Brian Leetch power-play goal against the Pittsburgh Penguins' Tom Barrasso at Madison Square Garden. The monumental point was a second assist on Leetch's goal. Gretzky led the attack into Pittsburgh's zone, deftly slipped the puck cross-ice to Matthieu Schneider, who directed it to Leetch, pinching on the play. Leetch went high over a sprawling Barrasso to tie the game 1–1. Ironically the Pittsburgh player who was off for tripping that led to Gretzky's final point was the same player who scored the overtime game winner—Jaromir Jagr. Yes, the goal-scoring torch had been passed.

7.25 D. An international game
According to Wayne Gretzky, his greatest match was Canada's 6–5 win over the Soviet Union in Game 2 of the 1987 Canada Cup. Gretzky set up five goals, including the double-overtime winner by Mario Lemieux. "Because of the competition and level of skill, that was the best game I ever played," Gretzky told *The Hockey News*. Canada won the best-of-three final series 2–1. No. 99 considers his greatest NHL game to be Game 7 of 1993's Western Conference final between Los Angeles and Toronto. On May 29, 1993, the Great One scored his record eighth career playoff hat trick to lead the Kings in a 5–4 do-or-die victory. The win brought L.A. to its first and last Stanley Cup finals. The Kings lost the Cup to Montreal.

7.26 B. Golf shoes
Wayne Gretzky received a number of retirement gifts, including a jet-black Mercedes from the New York Rangers, a leather sofa in the shape of a baseball glove from New York teammates after his final practice, and a pair of spikes from close friend and golfer Mark O'Meara. The timing was perfect for the golf shoes. "That kind of took the edge off it," No 99 said. "This is a great game, but it's a hard game. Time does something to you, and it's time."

7.27 C. Winning his first Stanley Cup
When Wayne Gretzky was asked in August 1995 to recount his top-10 hockey memories, he said his No. 1 highlight was "winning that first Cup." Today he might offer the 1998 Olympics or his retirement party in New York.

The Great One's Top-10 Hockey Memories

1. Winning the Stanley Cup for the first time in 1984
2. Scoring 50 goals in 39 games
3. Amassing 200 points in 1981–82
4. The first All-Star Game, teamed with idol Gordie Howe
5. Four-goal performance at the 1983 All-Star Game
6. Goal No. 802, to become NHL all-time scoring leader
7. Point No. 1,851, breaking Gordie Howe's all-time points record
8. The 1987 Canada Cup, teamed with Mario Lemieux
9. The first NHL goal: October 14, 1979
10. Edmonton's upset sweep of Montreal in 1981

SOLUTIONS TO GAMES

Game 1: CROSSWORD OF GREATNESS

Game 2: NO. 99'S FIRST STANLEY CUP

Game 3: MILESTONE TARGETS

H A N L O N

P E E T E R S

L I U T

B R O D E U R

F L Y E R S

R A N F O R D

M C L E A N

L O S   A N G E L E S

A N   E M P T Y   N E T   G O A L

Game 4: OTHER CLAIMS TO FAME

1. 1971: E. First major feature on Gretzky appears in Toronto's *Telegram*
2. 1981: D. Andy Warhol paints Gretzky's portrait
3. 1982: J. U.S. President Ronald Reagan jokes he would trade two draft choices and the state of Texas for Gretzky
4. 1983: I. Mattel introduces a Gretzky action figure
5. 1984: H. First Gretzky-inspired book hits the market: *Gretzky*
6. 1988: A. Gretzky proposes to Janet Jones
7. 1989: B. Gretzky appears on *Saturday Night Live*
8. 1989: F. An eight-foot-high statue of Gretzky is unveiled at Northlands Coliseum in Edmonton
9. 1994: G. Gretzky enlists a group of all-star friends to play in Europe during the NHL work stoppage
10. 1998: C. Gretzky is awarded the Order of Canada

Game 5: CLOSE BUT NO CIGAR

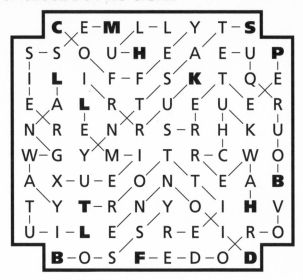

Game 6: NO. 99'S LAST STANLEY CUP

In Game 4 of the 1988 Stanley Cup finals between Edmonton and Boston, Boston Garden suddenly lost power. With the match tied 3–3 and minutes to play in the second period, the game was suspended. The series returned to Edmonton where the Oilers won their fourth Cup in five years.

ACKNOWLEDGMENTS

Many thanks go out to the following publishers and organizations for use of quoted material: *Gretzky: An Autobiography*, by Wayne Gretzky with Rick Reilly, published in 1990 by HarperCollins Canada; *The Hockey News*, for various excerpts, reprinted by permission of *The Hockey News*, a division of GTC Transcontinental Publishing, Inc; *The Hockey News*, for *The Great One: Wayne Gretzky, a Legend in Our Time;* the *National Post*, for various articles published in 1999; *The Sporting News*, a division of *Times-Mirror* magazine; and *Sports Illustrated*, for *Wayne Gretzky: A Tribute*.

Care has been taken to trace ownership of copyrighted material contained in this book. The publishers welcome any information that will enable them to rectify any reference or credit in subsequent editions.

The author gratefully acknowledges the help of Steve Dryden at *The Hockey News*; Bruce Bennett and Jim Leary of Bruce Bennett Studios; Gary Meagher and Benny Ercolani of the NHL; Phil Prichard at the Hockey Hall of Fame; *London Free Press* reporter John Herbert, who nicknamed Wayne Gretzky, the Great Gretzky (or the Great One, as he later became known); the staff at the McLellan-Redpath Library at McGill University; Rob Sanders, Terri Wershler and Robert Clements at Greystone Books; the many hockey writers and broadcasters who have made the game better through their work; and my editor Michael Carroll, fact checker Allen Bishop, graphic artist Peter van Vlaardingen and puzzle designer Adrian van Vlaardingen.

Finally, the following organizations provided photographs that appear on the pages indicated—Hockey Hall of Fame: 7, 28; Bruce Bennett Studios: 41, 48, 78, 92, 113, 118.